What Readers Are Saying About
Pragmatic Guide to Git

I'd heard a lot of the hype surrounding Git. It wasn't until I read Travis'
book that I learned why people are so enthusiastic about it. Travis does a
great job explaining the power of Git in a digestible format.

➤ **Ivo Jansch**
PHP evangelist, author, and founder, Egeniq.com

Git can be intimidating and frustrating to new users. *Pragmatic Guide to
Git* alleviates that pain with a straightforward, concise walk-through that
arms readers with exactly what they need to use Git productively.

➤ **Luigi Montanez**
Software developer, Sunlight Labs

This book is a must-have for anyone using Git or just getting started with
Git. It has saved me time in finding the best practices for managing my
Git repositories and will sit on my bookshelf as the go-to resource for
anything Git.

➤ **John Mertic**
Senior software engineer, SugarCRM

With two years of experience with Git, I thought I would have known most everything in *Pragmatic Guide to Git*. After reading it cover to cover, I learned that's not the case. It's a well-organized collection of useful Git techniques for all audiences.

➤ **Luke Pillow**
  Software engineer, pillowfactory.org

Pragmatic Guide to Git

Travis Swicegood

The Pragmatic Bookshelf

Dallas, Texas • Raleigh, North Carolina

Many of the designations used by manufacturers and sellers to distinguish their products are claimed as trademarks. Where those designations appear in this book, and The Pragmatic Programmers, LLC was aware of a trademark claim, the designations have been printed in initial capital letters or in all capitals. The Pragmatic Starter Kit, The Pragmatic Programmer, Pragmatic Programming, Pragmatic Bookshelf, PragProg and the linking *g* device are trademarks of The Pragmatic Programmers, LLC.

Every precaution was taken in the preparation of this book. However, the publisher assumes no responsibility for errors or omissions, or for damages that may result from the use of information (including program listings) contained herein.

Our Pragmatic courses, workshops, and other products can help you and your team create better software and have more fun. For more information, as well as the latest Pragmatic titles, please visit us at *http://pragprog.com*.

The team that produced this book includes:

Susannah Davidson Pfalzer (editor)
Potomac Indexing, LLC (indexer)
Kim Wimpsett (copyeditor)
Steve Peter (typesetter)
Janet Furlow (producer)
Juliet Benda (rights)
Ellie Callahan (support)

Printed in the United States of America.
ISBN-13: 978-1-934356-72-2
Printed on acid-free paper.
Book version: P3.0—January 2012

Contents

Part III — Organizing Your Repository with Branches and Tags

Part IV — Working with a Team

Part V — Branches and Merging Revisited

Part VI — Working with the Repository's History

Part VII — Fixing Things

Part VIII — Moving Beyond the Basics

Acknowledgments

Like any book, this is the result of much more than an author such as me sitting in front of their computer typing a bunch of words. Please give me a few minutes to thank those involved in bringing this book to you.

First, I'd like to thank a reader of my first book, who shot me an email that planted the seed that became this book.

Next, Dave, Andy, and the entire crew at Pragmatic Bookshelf have been great to work with a second time. Both books I've written for them have been gambles—first as a rookie author and then with this book as an author charting the territory of a new format—and they haven't blinked an eye.

My editor, Susannah Davidson Pfalzer, has been indispensable. She was always there with advice, tips, the occasional tough love, and an ever-optimistic attitude; every author should be so lucky.

Reviewers of early drafts of this book provided me with a tremendous amount of constructive feedback that helped shaped this book into what you're holding in your hands (or looking at on your computer's screen). Thanks to Joel Clermont, Javier Collado, Geoff Drake, Chad Dumler-Montplaisir, Wayne Huang, Michael Hunger, Ivo Jansch, Jerry Kuch, Johnathan Meehan, John Mertic, Luigi Montanez, Karl Pfalzer, Luke Pillow, Christophe Portneuve, Tom Sartain, Stefan Turalski, Tom Van Herreweghe, Matt Warren, and Nick Watts.

No acknowledgments for a book on an open source tool would be complete without acknowledging the work of the legion of volunteers who made the project possible. A huge debt is owed by all of us who use Git to the nearly 700 people who have contributed to the project.

My family and friends, in particular my wife (whom I'm lucky enough to count as both), have been amazing—as always. Without their support, and that of the rest of my family and friends, this book would not have happened.

Introduction

The world of version control systems (VCSs) has undergone a major shift over the past few years. Fast, reliable, and approachable distributed version control systems (DVCSs) such as Git have burst onto the scene and changed the landscape of open source software development and corporate software workflows.

This book is your guide to this new paradigm. It's not a complete reference; instead, it focuses on getting you up and running quickly. *Pragmatic Guide to Git* covers the 95 percent of Git that you'll use at least once a week, as well as a few tasks that will come in handy but aren't used as often.

Git started when the license of VCS software that the Linux kernel used to track changes was revoked. After investigating the other alternatives, Linus Torvalds decided he could write a better version control system in a few weeks than what currently existed, so he set off to do that.

Git, then in a very rough form, was the result of that two weeks of hacking together some shell scripts back in the spring of 2005. Linus had to calculate pieces of the commits by hand on the first few commits (commits are the changes Git tracks for you). Since those original hand-rolled commits, Git has become the leader in the field of DVCS.

Who Is This Book For?

This book is geared for someone new to Git who is looking to get up to speed quickly. This book is for you if you're status.untracked.start familiar with another VCS such as Subversion and are looking for a quick guide to the Git landscape or if you're a quick study and want a concise guide. It's organized by task to make it easy to translate from the task you need to accomplish to how the process works in Git.

If you've never used a version control system before and thought Subversion was something you did to overthrow governments, this book will get you up and running with Git. For much more detail on version control concepts, you should read *Pragmatic Version Control Using Git,*[1] my other book, as well.

How to Read This Book

This book is organized in parts to guide you from starting out through more complex situations, with each part broken down into tasks. Tasks follow a specific formula: the left page explains the task and the commands related to it, and the right page gives you the raw commands with a little bit of information about them and a cross-reference to related tasks.

You can read this book in paper form as an open book to see the tasks side by side, but it's also an excellent reference in digital form, especially when searching for a particular Git task.

If you're reading a digital version of this book on a computer with a large enough display, I recommend setting your reader to display two pages side by side instead of a single page. That gives you the same visual that's intended in the book.

On your first pass, I suggest that you read the introductions to each part. They give you a broad overview of how to approach each part of the Git workflow, as well as a synopsis of the tasks contained in that part.

Armed with high-level information, you can determine where to dive in. You can read this book from start to finish or cherry-pick the tasks relevant to what you're trying to accomplish.

The parts of this book are organized to walk you through the various phases of use in Git.

---

1.   http://pragprog.com/titles/tsgit/

- Part I, *Getting Started*, starts with the absolute basics — installing and configuring Git and creating your first repository.

- Part II, *Working with Git*, covers the basic commands you need as part of your day-to-day interaction with Git by yourself. These are the building blocks, and they're a must-read if this is your first time using Git.

- Part III, *Organizing Your Repository with Branches and Tags*, introduces branches, a powerful and central part of Git that's necessary for understanding how everything works together.

- Part IV, *Working with a Team*, covers the most powerful aspect of any VCS: collaborating with other developers. This part gets you up to speed on how to share your work with other developers and retrieve changes from them.

- Part V, *Branches and Merging Revisited*, builds on the information in Part III and teaches you how to handle it when things go wrong, as well as some of the more complex ways to handle merging and moving branches around.

- Part VI, *Working with the Repository's History*, introduces you to all the history you've been generating. Using this information, you can figure out what another developer (or maybe even you) was thinking when you made a particular change.

- Part VII, *Fixing Things*, shows you how Git can help you fix things in your repository — be that commits that need to be adjusted or finding bugs in your code.

- Part VIII, *Moving Beyond the Basics*, introduces you to a few concepts that don't fit into the normal everyday workflow but are useful when they're needed.

There are diagrams throughout this book. Whenever you see a circle, it represents a commit — with the exception of Figure 2, *Shared and distributed repository layout with three developers*, on page xix, where the circles represent repositories.

This matches the style used throughout the Git manual when it shows example repository structures to explain commands. In addition to the standard graphical diagrams throughout, in some places I've opted for a plain-text diagram to introduce you to the Git manual diagram style.

Throughout the book you'll see examples of the output you can expect Git to generate for a given command. Keep in mind that your output won't be exactly the same because of the way Git keeps track of commit IDs—more on that in a minute.

Several commands don't generate any output after they run successfully, though. For these commands, I include an empty prompt> after the successful command to show that there is no output.

The first reference to each new term includes an explanation of what the term means. If you read the book from start to finish, you'll know all of the terms from previous introductions to them.

Did you forget a term or are you using the book as a reference and not reading it straight through? You're covered there, too. You can refer to Appendix 1, *Glossary*, on page 131; there you'll get explanations of all the common—and some not so common—jargon you'll encounter in this book and in your adventures in Git.

What Version of Git to Use

I used the 1.7.*x* version of Git while writing the majority of this book. All of the commands as of this writing work with 1.7.2.1 and should work with the majority of Git 1.6.*x* versions.

The installation methods mentioned in Task 1, *Installing Git*, on page 4 all have recent versions of Git available, so make sure you're running a recent version, and you won't have any trouble following along. You can run git --version from the command line to see what version you have.

Before we dive into the tasks, let's talk a bit about Git and what makes it unique.

How Git Is Different

Git is a bit different from traditional version control systems. If you're coming to Git from another centralized system, this section explains some of the differences and gets you thinking in Git style.

Distributed vs. Centralized

There are generally two models in version control systems: centralized and distributed. Tools such as Subversion typically require a network connection to a centralized server. You make a change to your project and then commit that change, which is sent to the centralized server to track. Other developers can then immediately access your changes.

Distributed version control systems, such as Git, break the process of committing code and sharing it with others into two parts. You can commit your code to your local private repository without having to talk to a centralized server, removing the need to be connected to a network to make a change.

Private vs. Public Repositories

Each developer who is sharing code with other developers has at least two repositories: a private and a public repository. The private repository is the one that exists on your computer and is the one you make commits to.

Public repositories are the repository that you use to share your changes with other developers. Multiple developers might have access to push changes to the same public repository, or each developer may have their own public repositories.

You can push to and fetch from multiple repositories. This allows you to pull in changes from another developer who's working on the same project.

Commit IDs Instead of Revision Numbers

Centralized VCS have the benefit of having one system that doles out revision numbers. Because everyone is committing and sharing their code in one repository, that repository can control what numbers it assigns to a particular commit.

That model doesn't work in a decentralized system. Who's to say which commit is actually the second commit, me or you? Git uses commit IDs that are SHA-1 hashes instead. The hash is based on the code, what came before it, who made the commit, when they made it, and a few other pieces of metadata. The chances are incredibly small of there being two different commits with the same commit ID.

Forking Is Good

For the longest time, forking a project was a bad thing. It drained resources away from the main project, and merging changes between the two projects was time-consuming when possible.

Git's superior merge capabilities, rooted in its distributed nature, make merging changes from a "forked" repository trivial. In fact, the idea of forking is so ingrained in the Git community that one of the largest Git communities online, GitHub,[2] is built around the concept. To offer your changes, you fork a repository, commit your changes, and then ask the original developer to pull your changes in through a *pull request*.

Instead of an indicator of a project suffering from internal strife, the number of forks on a repository is considered the sign of an active community working on a project.

The Git Workflow

Working by yourself on a project with no version control, you hack a little, test it out and see whether it does what you want, tweak a few more lines of code, and repeat. Adding version control into the mix, you start committing those tweaks to keep a record of them. The high-level overview of Git's general workflow is shown in Figure 1, *The Git workflow*, on page xvii.

My Standard Workflow

My standard day working with Git goes something like this: I fetch all the changes from the other developers on my team to make sure I'm working with the latest code, and then I

---

2. http://github.com/

Start your day here

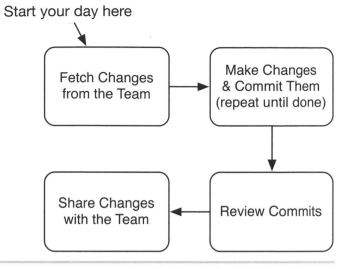

Figure 1— The Git workflow

start working on the user stories I have for the day. As I make changes, I create a handful of commits—a separate commit for each change that I make.

Occasionally, I end up with several separate changes that all need to be committed. I'll break out Git's patch mode, stage, and finally commit each set of changes separately.

Once I have the feature complete, I give the commits I've created a quick review to make sure all the changes are necessary. At this point I look for commits that can be combined and make sure they are in the most logical order.

Finally, once I have those commits ready, I share those commits by pushing them (*push* is the term for sending commits to another repository) back upstream to my public repository so the rest of the team can view them and integrate them with their repositories.

Small Teams with a Shared Repository

Many small teams use Git like a traditional version control system. They have one main repository that all the developers can send changes to, and each developer has their own private repository to track their changes in.

You make your changes locally; then when you're ready to share them with other developers, you push them back to the repository you all share.

If someone else has shared their changes since the last time you updated from the shared repository, you will get an error. You must first get the changes from the shared repository and integrate them into your repository through a process called *merging*. Once the changes are merged, you can push your changes to share with the rest of the team.

Git in Open Source

Each open source project has its own methods of accepting changes. Some projects use a fully distributed model where only one person can push changes to the main repository, and that person is responsible for merging changes from all the contributors into the main repository.

Having only one person capable of pushing changes is often too demanding a job for a large open source project. Many have a main repository that all of the *committers* can send changes to.

The main developers encourage people who are just starting out to fork their project—create a copy of the repository somewhere else—so the main developers and other members of the community can review their changes. If they're accepted, one of the main contributors merges them back into the project's repository.

These different scenarios constitute different repository layouts. Git allows several different layouts, and covering them deserves a section to itself.

Repository Layouts

The distributed nature of Git gives you a lot of flexibility in how you manage your repositories. Every person on your team has their own private repository—the repository that only that person can update. However, there are two distinct ways to handle public repositories. For a visual explanation of these layouts, see Figure 2, *Shared and distributed repository layout with three developers*, on page xix.

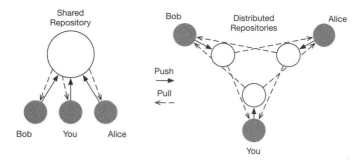

Gray circles are the private repositories; outlined circles are public repositories.

Figure 2— Shared and distributed repository layout with three developers.

One method is the fully distributed model. In this, each developer has their own public repository that the developer uses to publish their changes to. All the other developers on the team then pull changes from everyone else's repositories to keep current.

In practice, most teams have a lead developer who is responsible for making sure all the changes are integrated. This limits the number of repositories you and your team have to pull changes from to one, but it increases the workload on the person who has to integrate everyone's changes.

Another method is the shared repository model, where all developers can push to a *shared repository*. This resembles the standard centralized model and is often adopted by teams when they first start using Git—it requires the least amount of mental overhead when it comes to thinking about where a change is shared.

You can mix both of these as well to create a hybrid solution. Use a shared repository for all of the code that's ready for production, and each developer maintains their own public repository for sharing code that's still a work in progress. This is the model I've employed successfully at my company and that's used by many open source projects—push final changes to the main repository, and keep experimentation in your own repository.

Online Resources

Several online resources are available for this book. The book's website is the jumping-off point for all of them:

http://pragprog.com/titles/pg_git/

From here, you can view the errata (and add any errors you find) and head to the book's forum where you can discuss and ask questions—both about the book and about Git.

Now that you know what this book is about, let's get started.

Part I

Getting Started

Ready to get started with Git?[3] Git is an extremely powerful tool that's relatively easy to start using. Like all software, it requires installation and minimal setup before you can start using it.

Covered in this part:

- We start off with Task 1, *Installing Git*, on page 4 to handle installation. Git's heritage in the Linux world means it can be compiled directly from source, but there are other (easier) options for every major operating system.

- You need to tell Git a few configuration settings before you start using it, covered in Task 2, *Configuring Git*, on page 6.

- Now that Git is installed and configured, you start using it in Task 3, *Creating a New Repository*, on page 8. You learn how to create a completely new repository.

- Another way to start a Git repository is to create a clone of someone else's repository, covered in Task 4, *Creating a Local Copy of an Existing Repository*, on page 10.

Once you've made it through these basic steps, you'll be ready to start working with Git. Feel free to skim the following tasks if you already have Git installed and configured and have created a new repository or cloned an existing one.

---

3.   I promise, no more get/Git puns the rest of the book.

1   Installing Git

You can install Git in several different ways: by using one of the GUI installers, by using a package management system, or, in the time-honored Linux tradition that spawned Git, by compiling it from source.

Don't worry if you're not ready to start compiling software; all major operating systems provide alternatives to compiling Git yourself. For example, Ubuntu provides Git via its apt-get tool, so a few commands from the terminal are enough to get you going. Likewise, OS X users have the option of using MacPorts[5] or the new Homebrew[6] to handle the installation. Not to be left out, Windows users who use Cygwin[7] can also install it via Cygwin's setup.exe.

Windows and OS X users who prefer GUI installations have alternatives available as well. Windows users can use the msysGit[8] installer to get up and running, and OS X users can install Git using the Git OS X Installer[9] to install Git via a DMG.

The original way to install Git, which is still the best if you want to remain on the latest version, is to build it from source. The various dependencies can be hard to track down, especially if you plan on building the user manual. Tools like apt-get build-dep on Ubuntu are helpful for tracking down all of the dependencies.

Watch mixing installation tools. For example, if you use a Mac and have installed most of your software using MacPorts, stick with Mac-Ports; if you compile all your own software on Linux, now probably isn't the time to start using apt-get. Switching to Git provides you with enough learning opportunities, so be careful to guard that installing Git doesn't cause the yak to get a trim.[10]

---

5.   http://www.macports.org/
6.   http://github.com/mxcl/homebrew — Homebrew is relatively new tool that handles compiling software on a Mac. It stores all of its formulas, the instructions for installing software, in a Git repository.
7.   http://www.cygwin.com/
8.   http://code.google.com/p/msysgit/
9.   http://code.google.com/p/git-osx-installer/
10.   http://en.wiktionary.org/wiki/yak_shaving

➤ Compile Git from its source code.

Download the latest tarball from the Git website.[4]

```
prompt> tar -xjf git-YOUR-VERSION.tar.bz2
prompt> cd git-YOUR-VERSION
prompt> make
prompt> make install
```

You can compile the documentation from source as well. Replace the last two lines in the previous steps with this:

```
prompt> make all doc
prompt> make install install-doc
```

➤ Install Git on Ubuntu.

```
prompt> sudo apt-get install git-core
```

To install the user manual, do this:

```
prompt> sudo apt-get install git-doc
```

To install the Git to Subversion functionality, do this:

```
prompt> sudo apt-get install git-svn
```

You can use apt-get to handle all of the dependencies and then compile Git from source using the previous steps.

```
prompt> sudo apt-get build-dep git-core git-doc git-svn
```

➤ Install Git on OS X.

You can use MacPorts and install Git with SVN functionality:

```
prompt> sudo port install git-core +svn
```

There is also a Git Installer for OS X available on Google Code.

➤ Install on Windows.

Download latest msysGit installer from here:

```
http://code.google.com/p/msysgit/
```

Or, install as part of Cygwin's setup process.

---

4.   http://git-scm.com/

2   Configuring Git

Git requires some configuration to work. You must tell Git your name and your email address since there is no central repository to keep track of that information. Git uses both to calculate the commit ID—an SHA-1[11] hash—that identifies each commit.

The first two commands on the next page use --global to specify that they are configuration values for every repository you interact with on this machine. The configuration file is stored in ~/.gitconfig. You can edit the file directly in addition to using the git config command.

You can set every setting on a global or per-repository basis. By leaving --global out of the command, the settings will be stored in the repository's .git/config file.

You might want to set a few other useful configuration values while configuring Git. You can set color.ui to auto if you like to have your command-line interfaces colorized.

The auto setting tells Git to use color whenever it is generating output to be displayed but to render plain text whenever the output is being piped to another process. This makes it easy to output a raw diff—the changes between two versions of the file—to a file but still allows you to see the colorized diff when you view the output directly.

Finally, Git uses core.editor to specify a particular editor. Git launches an editor whenever you need to create a commit message, edit patches, and do a few other tasks.

Git doesn't require you to set the core.editor value, though. It tries to figure out what editor to use by checking the following values, in order: GIT_EDITOR environment variable; core.editor configuration value; VISUAL environment variable; EDITOR environment variable; and, finally, plain vi.

The value is the command-line script to launch your editor. In Windows, this is a bit tricky, but there's an excellent thread on Stack Overflow[12] that can help you get started.

---

11. http://en.wikipedia.org/wiki/SHA
12. http://j.mp/git-editor-on-windows

➤ Configure Git to know who you are.

```
prompt> git config --global user.name "Your Name"
prompt> git config --global user.email "user@domain.com"
prompt>
```

➤ Set the Git user for a specific repository.

```
prompt> cd /path/to/repository
prompt> git config user.name "Your Name"
prompt> git config user.email "user@domain.com"
prompt>
```

➤ Turn colors on wherever possible in the Git UI.

```
prompt> git config --global color.ui auto
prompt>
```

➤ Configure Git's editor.

```
prompt> git config --global core.editor /path/to/editor
prompt>
```

3   Creating a New Repository

Repositories in Git are stored on your local file system right alongside the code they track. You create a repository by typing git init in the directory that you want to start tracking files in.

You use two repositories in Git to collaborate with others: a private one and a public one. Your private repository—the one we're creating here—is where you do all your work. It's the repository with the working tree.

This two-tier system gives you the ability to track local experimental changes while only sharing changes via your public repository that are ready for others to work with. Be careful that you don't allow yourself to code in a cave, though. Hoarding all your changes until they are "just right" is the quickest way to harm a project. Share early; share often.

git init creates a .git directory in your current directory and initializes the Git repository inside that. Once you've initialized a repository, you still need to add and commit the files using git add (see Task 6, *Staging Changes to Commit,* on page 20) and git commit (see Task 7, *Committing Changes,* on page 22), respectively, but both of these require an initialized repository first. You have to initialize the repository only once.

Once you've initialized a repository, you have a *working tree* that you can interact with. The working tree is your view into what's stored in your repository. It typically represents the latest copy of what's stored in your repository.

➤ Create a repository.

```
prompt> mkdir some-repository
prompt> cd some-repository
prompt> git init
```

For example, to create a repository called widgets in the /work directory, use this:

```
prompt> mkdir /work/widgets
prompt> cd /work/widgets
prompt> git init
Initialized empty Git repository in /work/widgets/.git/
```

➤ Create a repository in an existing directory, and add all files from that directory.

```
prompt> cd /path/to/some/directory
prompt> git init
prompt> git add .
prompt> git commit -m "some commit message"
```

For example, to create a repository inside an existing directory called /work/existing-widget, use this:

```
prompt> cd /work/existing-widget
prompt> git init
Initialized empty Git repository in /work/existing-widget/.git/
prompt> git add .
prompt> git commit -m "initial commit"
[master (root-commit) 6e477fa] initial commit
 101 files changed, 4083 insertions(+), 0 deletions(-)
 create mode 100644 AUTHORS
 ... and 100 more files ...
```

Related Tasks:

- Task 4, *Creating a Local Copy of an Existing Repository*, on page 10
- Task 7, *Committing Changes*, on page 22
- Task 12, *Sharing Changes*, on page 32
- Task 44, *Initializing Bare Repositories*, on page 128

4   Creating a Local Copy of an Existing Repository

You need to create a clone of a remote repository to start making changes to it. The git clone command initializes a new repository on your computer and fetches the entire history—all the changes that have been tracked during the life of that repository. After it's complete, you can start making changes to the files in your local working tree and tracking commits locally.

Sometimes you don't need the entire history of the repository. You don't always need the last ten years of changes—the last year's might suffice. You can use the --depth parameter to limit how many revisions you fetch. This is called a *shallow repository*.

There are a few limitations to this type of repository clone. For example, you can't create another clone from it. There is a place for these clones, however. Say you want to submit a patch—a change—to a project with a long history. You only need the recent changes to show your change against, so a shallow repository is perfect.

Depending on how the firewall on your computer or local area network (LAN) is configured, you might get an error trying to clone a remote repository over the network. Git uses SSH by default to transfer changes over the network, but it also uses the Git protocol (signified by having git:// at the beginning of the URI) on port 9418. Check with your local network administrator to make sure communication on ports 22—the port SSH communicates on—and 9418 are open on your local network if you have trouble communicating with a remote repository.

You use git clone to fetch changes when a repository already exists, but you don't have to clone a repository to work with a remote repository. Remote repositories are repositories that you can talk to, generally over a network, to push and pull changes from. You can initialize a new repository, like we talked about in Task 3, *Creating a New Repository*, on page 8, and then add a remote repository later with the git remote command (see Task 19, *Adding and Removing Remotes*, on page 60).

➤ Clone a repository.

```
prompt> git clone some-repository
... example ...
prompt> git clone git://github.com/tswicegood/bobby-tables.git
Cloning into bobby-tables...
remote: Counting objects: 39, done.
remote: Compressing objects: 100% (25/25), done.
remote: Total 39 (delta 16), reused 26 (delta 9)
Receiving objects: 100% (39/39), 39.23 KiB, done.
Resolving deltas: 100% (16/16), done.
```

➤ Clone a repository into a specific path.

```
prompt> git clone some-repository  some-path
... example ...
prompt> git clone git://github.com/tswicegood/bobby-tables.git btbls
Cloning into btbls...
remote: Counting objects: 39, done.
remote: Compressing objects: 100% (25/25), done.
remote: Total 39 (delta 16), reused 26 (delta 9)
Receiving objects: 100% (39/39), 39.23 KiB, done.
Resolving deltas: 100% (16/16), done.
```

➤ Create a shallow clone with the last fifty commits.

```
prompt> git clone --depth 50  some-repository
```

➤ These are valid Git repository URIs.

```
user@ssh host:path_to_repo
git://some_domain/path_to_repo
http://some_domain/path_to_repo/
https://some_domain/path_to_repo/path/to/repo
```

Related Tasks:

Part II

Working with Git

Now that you have Git and your repository set up, it's time to start learning how to interact with Git. A handful of commands are all you need to get you through most tasks. Once you finish the tasks in this part, you'll know them all.

As we saw in the introduction, the workflow in Git is different from other version control systems and definitely different from working without any version control system. Each time you make a change you want to track, you need to commit it.

The workflow goes like this. First, create your repository—either create a new repository or clone an existing one. Then make some changes, test that they do what you want, commit those changes, make some more changes, and so on. Finally, you share those changes when they're ready.

One thing to keep in mind when working with a distributed version control system (DVCS) like Git is that committing a change and sharing that change are two different processes. This is different from centralized VCS such as Subversion and CVS, where the two actions are synonymous.

This separation provides you with a lot of freedom. You can experiment locally, try a whole bunch of things, and then share the best solution, but to paraphrase an old uncle, "With great freedom comes great responsibility."

Lots of small, discrete changes that touch very specific portions of the code are better than a few monolithic changes. Make sure you don't sit on a whole bunch of changes until they're perfect. First, they'll *never* be perfect. There's always something else to refactor and abstract away. Second, the bigger the change becomes, the harder it becomes to fully understand, review, and test.

Third, it makes tracking down bugs later easier. Tools such as git bisect (see Task 39, *Finding Bugs with bisect*, on page 114) make finding which commit introduced a bug easy. Smaller commits mean that once you know which commit caused the bug, you can figure out the exact change that much faster.

We've already covered how to create a new repository or clone an existing one (git init and git clone in Task 3, *Creating a New Repository*, on page 8 and Task 4, *Creating a Local Copy of an Existing Repository*, on page 10, respectively). Making changes and testing are up to you and how you interact with the code in your project. Seeing what changes need to be committed is where we pick up. The tasks in this part are ordered roughly the same way you'll use them in Git.

Covered in this part:

- The first thing is seeing what has changed. We cover this in Task 5, *Seeing What Has Changed*, on page 18, which shows you how to compare your working tree with what the repository knows about.

- After you know what has changed, then you need to stage the changes you want to commit. This is covered in Task 6, *Staging Changes to Commit*, on page 20.

- The changes are staged; now it's time to commit them. Task 7, *Committing Changes*, on page 22 shows you how to create a commit and add a log message to it.

- With any project, files will be generated that you don't need to commit. Task 8, *Ignoring Files*, on page 24 teaches you how to tell Git to ignore those files.

- What happens when you accidentally stage a file you didn't mean to or you decide that you want to get rid of a change that you made to a file before committing it? Task 9, *Undoing Uncommitted Changes*, on page 26 covers how to undo those staged changes so you don't accidentally commit something.

- Files sometimes need to change where they live. A new project layout is adopted, or files or directories are renamed. Task 10, *Moving Files in Git*, on page 28 shows you how to handle these inevitable changes.

- Likewise, some files or directories outlive their usefulness. Since the repository keeps a record of all files that it has ever tracked, you can delete those old files without worrying about not having them to reference later if you need to do so. Task 11, *Deleting Files in Git*, on page 30 shows you how.

- Finally, Task 12, *Sharing Changes*, on page 32 is a whirlwind tour of how to share changes with other developers. It's done at 30,000 feet and is enough to get you started. A lot more about collaboration is covered in Part IV, *Working with a Team*.

Now, let's dive into the specifics.

5   Seeing What Has Changed

Your local repository tracks changes. Before you start committing just anything, you need to see what changes exist between your working tree and your repository and what changes are staged and ready to commit. git status is the tool for the job.

git status has several different outputs, depending on what's in your working tree. The example on the next page is from one of my repositories, and it contains all three types of outputs: staged changes, changes to known files, and untracked files. Let's go over them in reverse order of how they appear on the next page—the order of least important to most.

Starting at lines 14 and ending at 17, Git outputs the files and paths that it doesn't know anything about—the files that you haven't told Git about yet. This section has the header Untracked files before it starts, and if you turned on color output like we discussed in Task 2, *Configuring Git*, on page 6, it displays the files and paths in red.

Next up are the files that Git knows about but that have changed. These are listed between lines 8 and 12 and are preceded by Changed but not updated. Like untracked files, these show up as red if you have colors configured.

Finally, the top section listed between lines 3 and 6 shows what files you would commit if you ran git commit right now. For more on committing, flip to Task 7, *Committing Changes*, on page 22. Files in this section show up as green if you turned colors on and are preceded by Changes to be committed.

Depending on the state of your repository, the output from git status might contain any of those sections or none at all. It adapts itself as needed.

➤ What the status of a new repository looks like.

If you just created a repository using git init, this is what your repository looks like:

```
prompt> git status
# On branch master
#
# Initial commit
#
nothing to commit (create/copy files and use "git add" to track)
```

➤ What git status looks like in a repository with changes.

git status requires a repository with some changes in its working tree to see the various output. The following is the output of git status on my local Castanaut repository:

```
Line 1  prompt> git status
        # On branch master #
        # Changes to be committed: #
        #   (use "git reset HEAD <file>..." to unstage)
      5 #
        #         modified:   castanaut.gemspec #
        #
        # Changed but not updated: #
        #   (use "git add <file>..." to update what will be committed)
     10 #   (use "git checkout -- <file>..." to discard changes in ...
        #
        #         modified:   README.txt #
        #
        # Untracked files: #
     15 #   (use "git add <file>..." to include in what will be ...
        #
        #         pkg/ #
```

➤ What git status looks like with no changes.

```
prompt> git status
# On branch master
nothing to commit (working directory clean)
```

Related Tasks:

- Task 3, *Creating a New Repository*, on page 8
- Task 6, *Staging Changes to Commit*, on page 20
- Task 7, *Committing Changes*, on page 22

| 6 | Staging Changes to Commit |

Git uses a two-step process to get changes into the repository. The first step is staging changes through git add. Staging a change adds it to the *index*, or staging area. This sits between the working tree—your view of the repository—and the actual repository.

Through the staging area, you can control what is staged from the most coarse-grained—adding everything within the repository—down to editing the changes, line by line.

First you can select individual files or paths to add by calling git add and passing the filename or path as the parameter. Git adds everything under a path if you provide that. It uses standard shell-style wildcards, so wildcards work: base.* matches base.rb and base.py.

Another quick way to add all files is the -A parameter. This adds all the files inside the repository that are not explicitly ignored (see Task 8, *Ignoring Files*, on page 24). Closely related, you can add files that have changed using the -u parameter. It doesn't add any new files, though, only files that have already been tracked and have modifications in them.

You can control which parts of a file you commit using the -p parameter. Running this, you're presented with each section of the file that has changed, and you're given the opportunity to add or skip it. You can stage the change by pressing y or skip a change with n. s lets you break the change into smaller pieces. This and a few other options aren't always available. You can press ? inside patch mode to get a list of all the commands and what they do.

Taking the control a step further, you can directly edit the changes that are being staged by using the -e parameter. This opens the diff in your configured editor (we talked about that in Task 2, *Configuring Git*, on page 6). Your editor has the file in a diff format—additions are prefixed with +, and removals are prefixed with -.

One quirk of Git is that it can't track empty directories (at least as of version 1.7.2.1). There's a reason for this in the underlying architecture and the way Git tracks data in the repository, but that's a bigger topic than this page allows for. To track an "empty" directory, you can add an empty dot file (a file beginning with a dot). An empty .gitignore works (see Task 8, *Ignoring Files*, on page 24). I use .include_in_git.

➤ Stage an entire file to commit.

```
prompt> git add path/to/file
... or ...
prompt> git add path/
... or everything under the current directory ...
prompt> git add .
prompt>
```

➤ Add all files in the current repository.

```
prompt> git add -A|--all
prompt>
```

➤ Add all tracked files that have been changed.

```
prompt> git add -u|--update
prompt>
```

➤ Choose which changes to commit.

```
prompt> git add -p|--patch
... or a specific file ...
prompt> git add -p path/to/file
prompt>
```

➤ Open the current diff in the editor.

```
prompt> git add -e
... or a specific file ...
prompt> git add -e path/to/file
prompt>
```

Related Tasks:

- Task 9, *Undoing Uncommitted Changes*, on page 26
- Task 5, *Seeing What Has Changed*, on page 18
- Task 7, *Committing Changes*, on page 22

7   Committing Changes

Git tracks changes to your repository through commits, which you make with the git commit command. It is the workhorse of Git and something you'll use a ton.

Prior to most commits, you need to stage the files you want to commit using the git add. You can use it to stage specific changes, portions of files, and other things that are covered in more detail in Task 6, *Staging Changes to Commit*, on page 20.

Each commit requires a commit message. You can use -m and a string in quotation marks as your message or use Git's editor to write a message. There's more information on the editor in Task 2, *Configuring Git*, on page 6. You can specify multiple paragraphs by specifying multiple -m parameters.

You can avoid git add and commit every change in your working tree with the -a parameter. It commits everything you have staged and all the changes to your working tree.

Because Git breaks committing and sharing into two separate tasks, you can change commits that haven't been shared. We've all accidentally committed a file that we weren't supposed to and realized the second after we hit Enter that there was a problem with the commit. You can amend your commit with the --amend parameter. You can add -C HEAD (HEAD points to the latest commit in your branch) to the call to reuse the commit's original log message if you don't need to change it. There's more on --amend in Task 35, *Fixing Commits*, on page 106.

➤ Stage and commit changes.

```
prompt> git add <some file>
prompt> git commit -m "Some message"
[master a276f08] Some message
 1 files changed, 2 insertions(+), 0 deletions(-)
```

➤ Commit all modified files.

```
prompt> git commit -m "Some message" -a
[master 5d251db] Some message
 1 files changed, 1 insertions(+), 0 deletions(-)
```

➤ Commit and launch editor for commit message.

```
prompt> git add <some file>
prompt> git commit
```

Related Tasks:

8 Ignoring Files

Software projects generate a lot of cruft. Some of it you don't need to commit. For example, I do a lot of work in Python, which leaves a ton of .pyc files laying around, and I edit using MacVim, which creates a swap file for each file that you're editing. We don't need or want these files cluttering up our repository or showing up in git status. That's where the .gitignore and friends comes in.

Each line of the .gitignore is scanned, and any matches it finds are ignored by Git. Your .gitignore file is inside your repository, so you can track it like any other file. You can put it at the top level of your repository, and in that case the rules cascade through all subdirectories. You can also use subdirectory-specific .gitignore, and those rules will only apply to files and directories inside that subdirectory.

Sometimes you don't want to commit your .gitignore file to your repository. Maybe you're contributing to an open source project—there's no need to add your *.swp to the project-wide .gitignore. You have two options in this case: use the .git/info/excludes file or add the ignore cases to your global excludesfile.

The .git/info/excludes is the same as a .gitignore file, except it's not tracked by Git since it's inside the .git directory. It's useful for excluding files that are specific to a project without adding a .gitignore file to the repository.

For files that you want to ignore in every repository on your computer, you can set the core.excludesfile configuration value to point to a file that contains your global ignore rules. It follows the same format as the .gitignore and .git/info/excludes files.

➤ Ignore a specific file and/or path called cache.

Add the following to .gitignore:

```
cache
```

➤ Ignore all .swp files from Vim.

Add the following to .gitignore:

```
*.swp
```

➤ Set up a global excludes file.

Your excludes file can exist anywhere you want on your computer. The following example puts it in your home directory in the .gitignore file:

```
prompt> git config --global core.excludesfile \
    ~/.gitignore
```

I have the following my ~/.gitignore since I'm on a Mac and use Vim:

```
.DS_Store
*.swp
```

9   Undoing Uncommitted Changes

Git's two-step process for tracking a commit means you can have files that are staged for commit that you're not ready to commit. You use git reset HEAD or git rm --cached depending on the circumstance.

Scenario 1: You staged a change to a file and want to unstage it—use git reset HEAD. This is the most common use. You're telling Git, "Change the index—the staging area—to the latest version of this file."

Scenario 2: You have a new file that's been staged that you don't want to commit now—use git rm --cached. Normally, git rm is used to remove files from your repository, but adding the --cached option tells Git to leave your working tree alone.

Another common problem is making changes that you want to undo completely. You can use git checkout to do this, but be careful. git checkout happily removes all untracked changes from a file or directory. You can't get those changes back if they were never tracked by Git.

➤ Unstage a modified file that's been staged.

For example, to undo changes to cache.py, use this:

```
prompt> git reset HEAD -- cache.py
Unstaged changes after reset:
M       cache.py
```

If you're not familiar with command-line programs, you might not recognize that --. It tells Git that all arguments are done and that the rest are files or paths. It's useful when files and branch or tag names clash.

➤ Undo all uncommitted changes to a file.

Warning: Doing this deletes files and cannot be undone.

```
prompt> git checkout -- cache.py
```

Related Tasks:

- Task 36, *Reverting Commits*, on page 108
- Task 37, *Resetting Staged Changes and Commits*, on page 110

10   Moving Files in Git

Performing tasks such as reorganizing files, changing file formats, and so on, requires that files and sometimes entire directories get moved. git mv handles this for you.

You provide it with two options: the name of the original file and the new name. This works on files, directories, or symlinks — anything Git can track.

You can move files, directories, and symlinks into other directories as well. Provide git mv a directory as the second option, and you're set.

Git stages the change for you after you call git mv. You must call git commit after git mv to make the move permanent.

git mv won't overwrite an existing file; it displays an error instead. You can override this behavior by providing --force (or -f). Be careful, though, because this makes Git overwrite the existing file. That's dangerous if the existing file you're overwriting isn't tracked by Git. You have no way of getting that file back.

➤ Move a file or directory.

For example, to move README.md to README.rst, use this:

```
prompt> git mv README.md README.rst
prompt> git commit -m "Changed README from Markdown to ReSTructured text"
[master f810d86] Changed README from Markdown to ReSTructured text
 1 files changed, 0 insertions(+), 0 deletions(-)
 rename README.md => README.rst (100%)
```

➤ Move a file or directory into another directory.

```
prompt> git mv README.rst docs/
prompt> git commit -m "Moved README into docs/ directory"
[master 99a0de8] Moved README into docs/ directory
 1 files changed, 0 insertions(+), 0 deletions(-)
 rename README.rst => docs/README.rst (100%)
```

Related Tasks:

- Task 6, *Staging Changes to Commit*, on page 20
- Task 7, *Committing Changes*, on page 22

11   Deleting Files in Git

Files and directories sometimes outlive their usefulness. You can remove them from your working tree and tell Git to quit tracking them using the git rm command.

This doesn't remove the file from your repository's history; it removes it only from your working tree going forward. You can always go back in the history of the repository and see the files or directories that have been removed.

You call git rm and provide it with a filename to tell Git to remove it (or a standard shell pattern—*.php matches all files that end in .php). You don't have to provide the --, but it's necessary if you're trying to remove a file that conflicts with a command-line option. It tells Git that you're done providing options, and everything else is a file.

You must provide the -r option if you are deleting a directory and all the files under it. It tells Git to recursively delete all the files starting at the provided directory.

Like most other actions in Git, git rm requires git commit to finalize its action. git rm stages the removal, and git commit finalizes it.

You can undo a git rm before you make a commit through a two-step process. First, you have to reset the index using git reset HEAD. Be sure to provide the filename if you want to leave other staged files alone. Second, check out the file from the repository to restore it using git checkout -- path/to/file.

git rm attempts to keep you from accidentally deleting a file that has changes that have not been committed. You can override this behavior with -f, but be careful. Forcing Git to delete the file removes the file and all traces of the changes that haven't been committed yet.

➤ **Delete a file from Git.**

To delete a file called outdated.py, use this:

```
prompt> git rm -- outdated.py
rm 'outdated.py'
prompt> git commit -m "remove outdated.py"
[master 42010bf] remove outdated.py
 1 files changed, 0 insertions(+), 17 deletions(-)
 delete mode 100644 outdated.py
```

➤ **Delete a directory from Git.**

To delete a directory called old/, use this:

```
prompt> git rm -r -- old/
rm 'old/outdated.py'
prompt> git commit -m "remove the old/ directory"
[master ddbd005] remove the old/ directory
 1 files changed, 0 insertions(+), 17 deletions(-)
 delete mode 100644 old/outdated.py
```

➤ **Get a directory back after deleting it but before committing it.**

This example uses the previous example where old/ is deleted using git rm, but before the staged deletes are committed. There are two steps. First, reset the index:

```
prompt> git reset HEAD -- old/
Unstaged changes after reset:
M        old/outdated.py
```

Second, check out the files from the repository:

```
prompt> git checkout -- old/
```

➤ **Force a file to be removed.**

```
prompt> git rm -f -- outdated.py
rm 'outdated.py'
```

Related Tasks:

- Task 9, *Undoing Uncommitted Changes*, on page 26
- Task 10, *Moving Files in Git*, on page 28

12   Sharing Changes

Remember that Git is different from most traditional version control systems; committing a change and sharing that change are two distinct tasks. Committing changes is covered in detail in Task 7, *Committing Changes*, on page 22; this task gives you a quick cheat sheet for the various tasks you need to perform to collaborate with others. For more detail on these steps, see Part IV, *Working with a Team*.

Once you have a local clone (see Task 4, *Creating a Local Copy of an Existing Repository*, on page 10) or have set up a remote after initializing your repository (see Task 19, *Adding and Removing Remotes*, on page 60), you need to fetch changes from the remote repository to keep your local branches (we'll cover what branches are in just a second in Part III, *Working with Branches*) in sync using git fetch. After fetching changes, you must merge those changes using any of the methods covered in Part III. Fetching is covered in more detail in Task 20, *Retrieving Remote Changes*, on page 62.

You can also fetch changes and merge them at the same time using git pull. It fetches the changes and then merges them into the current branch. You can specify the --rebase parameter to have Git rebase your local branch on top of the remote changes (see Task 16, *Rewriting History by Rebasing*, on page 48). Pulling is covered in more detail in Task 21, *Retrieving Remote Changes, Part II*, on page 64.

Sending changes back to a remote repository to share is done via the git push command. Consider it the inverse of git pull; it sends your changes to the remote repository and merges those changes into the remote branch via a fast-forward merge, which is a merge where both branches share a common ancestor and only the branch being merged in has changes in it.

Don't worry if parts of this sound like Greek. This is a high-level overview without diving into the specifics. The next two parts are going to fill in all the missing pieces.

➤ 1. Set up the remote repository.

   • You clone a repository. Or...

   • You add a remote to an existing repository.

➤ 2a. Fetch changes from a remote repository.

```
prompt> git fetch <remote name>
... then merge the changes into your work ...
```

➤ 2b. Pull changes from a remote repository.

```
prompt> git pull <remote name>
... pull from a repository you cloned ...
prompt> git pull origin
... pull, but rebase your local changes on top
... of the remote change instead of merging them
prompt> git pull --rebase origin <remote branch name>
```

➤ 3. Push changes to a remote repository.

```
prompt> git push <remote name> <branch name>
```

Related Tasks:

Part III

Organizing Your Repository with Branches and Tags

Now that you have the basics down, it's time to learn about branches. Branches allow you to segregate different lines of development. They're integral how Git works, so having a good conceptual understanding of what they are is crucial to becoming proficient with Git.

Version control systems of yesterday had poor support for branches and even worse support for merging those branches back together. Git changes this. In fact, one of the most compelling features of Git is its ability to easily handle creating branches and gracefully merge them back together.

Branches track changes to multiple versions of a project. For example, you might be finishing up version 1.0 and already starting on new features for version 1.1. Using branches, you can keep the code from version 1.0 isolated so new features from 1.1 don't accidentally slip into the version that is getting ready to release.

You give branches names, making it easier track them based on their name, rather than some commit ID. master is the name of the default branch that Git uses. All your commits so far in this book have been in that branch. You can create as many branches as you want.

Branches in Git are relatively simplistic—they're simply a text file inside the repository that marks the latest commit in the branch. Treating branches as pointers makes operations with branches painless and fast.

There are several different ways to approach using branches. One approach is the *topic branch*. You can use this style of branch to work on a specific feature, fix a bug, or deal with any other "topic." Once it's complete, then you merge the finished changes back into your master branch.

Another common type of branch is the *release branch*, the type of branch mentioned earlier. You create release branches as you approach a release in your project. They're useful when you or other members on your team are working on multiple versions of your project.

You can create a branch called release_v1.0 for the 1.0 version to isolate that release from features that aren't supposed to ship until version 1.1. Work on version 1.1 continues like normal in the master branch, and any changes from the final work on version 1.0 get merged back into master.

You can use tags to mark milestones in your project, such as releases. Tags are similar to branches, except they are read-only. Once you create a tag, you can't change it. Well, that's almost true, but for now consider them completely unchangeable.

Branches and tags are not shared by default. Like commits, you're given the ability to decide which branches and tags to share with other developers and when.

Branches in Git are pointers to a specific commit in your repository's history. Since each commit knows about its parent (or parents), Git can reconstruct what's in a branch by looking at the latest commit in that branch and walking the history backward to find all the ancestors. This simplified approach to branches makes them quick to create, rename, merge, and even delete.

You occasionally have to merge changes between branches to keep from duplicating the same work in different branches. Git makes this easy by tracking which commits have been merged between branches for you. Many modern VCS do not do this at all or do it poorly.

Git can employ several different *merge strategies* to merge branches together. The first is the *fast-forward merge*. Fast-forwards are performed when two conditions are met: when the branch you are merging in is being merged back into the branch it was created from and when the original branch hasn't had any new commits since the branch was

Before a Fast-Forward Merge

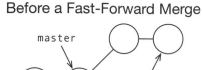

After a Fast-Forward Merge

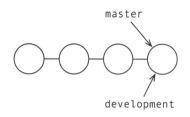

Figure 3— Before and after a fast-forward merge

created. For an example, check out Figure 3, *Before and after a fast-forward merge*, on page 39.

Fast-forward merges do not actually create anything new in the repository. They "fast-forward" the branch pointer to the new location.

Recursive merges are used by default when both the branches have commits that are not in the other branch. Git creates a *merge commit* that has two parent commits— the latest commit in each branch (see Figure 4, *Before and after a recursive merge*, on page 40).

Another way to get information from one branch into another is through rebasing the branch. Rebasing is a powerful tool in Git that's often misunderstood, which is understandable—there's no corollary in traditional VCS. It's best explained with an example workflow.

Consider the following example.

Before a Recursive Merge

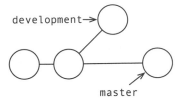

After a Recursive Merge

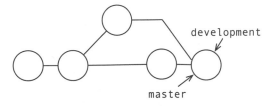

Figure 4— Before and after a recursive merge

Rebasing Changes

You start your morning by pulling in all the changes from the company's shared repository and then start working. During the morning, your co-worker pushes some commits upstream. When you try to push the commits you've made, you get an error. You now have two options. You can fetch the changes and do the following:

1. Merge them into your local branch, creating a merge commit.

2. Rebase your local branch on top of the remote branch.

Rebasing takes the commits you made this morning and then replays them, one by one, starting on the other branch. You can do this to keep the appearance of a continuous stream of development instead of having a bunch of merge commits scattered throughout your repository's history.

Now, let's see what's covered in this part:

*   Before you can use branches, you must create them. You will learn how to do that in Task 13, *Creating and Switching Branches*, on page 42.

- Keeping track of your branches requires that you be able to see what branches you have. Task 14, *Viewing Branches*, on page 44 covers the commands you need to know in order to see the branches you have in your repository.

- Having multiple branches to separate work on your project into different areas is useful only if you can merge the changes all back together. You learn this in Task 15, *Merging Commits Between Branches*, on page 46.

- No coverage of merging is complete without talking about rebasing. Rebasing is often misunderstood and feared, so Task 16, *Rewriting History by Rebasing*, on page 48 gets you comfortable with the mechanics of rebasing.

- Branches often outlive their intended use. Once you no longer need a branch, you can then delete it using the methods described in Task 17, *Deleting Branches*, on page 50.

- Finally, you need to be able to mark milestones in your branches. We cover that in Task 18, *Tagging Milestones*, on page 52.

At first glance, it might seem odd that branches—generally considered an advanced topic in most version control systems—are covered before discussing how to collaborate with a team. There is a reason for this. Remotes in Git are read-only branches. Once you know how to work with a branch, you know how to interact with a remote repository minus a couple of extra commands we'll cover when we get there.

13   Creating and Switching Branches

Git's branches enable you to separate experimentation from production-ready code. Git's convention is to treat the master branch as its main line of code. You can rename it to anything you want, but it's a good idea to keep with the convention.

You can create a new branch using the git branch command and providing it at least one additional parameter: the name of the branch you want to create. This uses your current location in the repository as the place to create the branch from.

You can also create branches starting at points in the history of the repository. Provide git branch with the name of the new branch you want to create followed by the commit ID or branch or tag name to create a branch at that point.

Following the "do one thing, do it well" idiom, git branch just creates the branch; you have to switch to it. You can use the git checkout command to *check out* the new branch.

Creating a new branch and checking it out immediately is common in Git. You can do both actions with one command: git checkout -b. Like git branch, it requires at least one parameter—the name of the new branch—and takes an optional second parameter specifying the point to create it from.

Tracking branches store additional metadata information about the relationship between two branches. The most common tracking branch is a local branch that tracks a remote branch (something Git does for you by default). The additional metadata is used by other commands, such as git push and git status, to provide additional functionality.

➤ Create a new branch from current place in the repository.

```
prompt> git branch <new branch name>
... example ...
prompt> git branch new
prompt>
```

➤ Create a new branch from another branch, tag, or commit.

```
prompt> git branch <new branch name> <starting point>
... example ...
prompt> git branch newer 99a0de8
prompt>
```

➤ Check out a different branch, tag, and so on.

```
prompt> git checkout <branch>
... example ...
prompt> git checkout newer
Switched to branch 'newer'
```

➤ Create a branch and check it out at the same time.

```
prompt> git checkout -b <new branch> [<starting point>]
... example ...
prompt> git checkout -b newest 64648c9
Switched to branch 'newest'
```

➤ Create a branch with or without tracking.

Using a remote branch as your <starting point> implies that --track is on.
Use --no-track to turn it off.

```
prompt> git branch --track <new branch> [<starting point>]
prompt> git branch --no-track <new branch> [<starting point>]
prompt>
```

Related Tasks:

- Task 14, *Viewing Branches,* on page 44
- Task 15, *Merging Commits Between Branches,* on page 46
- Task 16, *Rewriting History by Rebasing,* on page 48
- Task 29, *Moving Branches,* on page 84

14   Viewing Branches

You need to be able to see what branches your repository has in it so you can switch between them. You can use a visualization tool such as gitk[13] or GitX.[14] You can use git branch to get the same information, however.

You can view local, remote, or all branches depending on which parameters you pass to git branch. Calling git branch by itself shows you your local branches. You can add either the -r parameter or the -a parameter to view only the remote branches or all the branches, respectively.

Your current branch always has an asterisk before it in the output from git branch. It's colored green if you turned on color output (see Task 2, *Configuring Git*, on page 6). Likewise, remote branches are colored red if colors are on.

One gotcha with remote branches is that the output from git branch -a shows their name with a remotes/ prefix. git branch -r doesn't. You can use either name with commands that require a branch name.

It's useful to see what branches have or have not been merged into the current branch. You can see that by using the --merged and --no-merged parameters.

It's also useful to be able to find out which branches contain a particular commit. For example, you can track which branches contain a commit that has a known bug in it by using the --contains parameter.

---

13.   Gitk is a cross-platform application written in tcl/tk that ships with Git.
14.   A Mac-only clone of Gitk that is designed to be more "Mac-like." It's available from http://gitx.frim.nl/.

➤ View all local branches.

```
prompt> git branch
  master
  new
  newer
* newest
```

➤ View all remote branches.

```
prompt> git branch -r
  origin/master
```

➤ View all branches.

```
prompt> git branch -a
  master
  new
  newer
* newest
  remotes/origin/master
```

➤ View all that are or are not merged into the current branch.

```
prompt> git branch --merged
prompt> git branch --no-merged
```

➤ View all branches that contain a particular commit.

```
prompt> git branch --contains <commit id>
```

Related Tasks:

• Task 13, *Creating and Switching Branches*, on page 42
• Task 15, *Merging Commits Between Branches*, on page 46

15   Merging Commits Between Branches

You have to merge changes from another branch into your current branch in order to be able to use them. The simplest way to do this is through git merge.

git merge takes two options: the name of the other branch you want to merge and the optional local branch you want to merge into. You can leave off the current branch when you're merging changes into your current branch.

By default, git merge commits the merged changes if they can be successfully merged. You can short-circuit this with the --no-commit option. This is useful when you want to review, and possibly edit, the changes from the merge before making a commit.

We touched on how Git attempts to merge commits in the introduction to Part III. Fast-forward merges are often useful, but sometimes you want to log that a merge happened. This is common in projects when a big feature that was developed in a separate branch is merged in; it provides a single commit you can revert if it needs to be removed in the future. You can do this with the --no-ff option. It forces Git to create a merge commit, showing that the two branches were merged.

Another extra you can add when merge commits are created is the --log option. Traditional merge log messages contain Merge branch 'development'. There are two ways you change this. First, you can add the --log, which adds the subject line from each commit to the merge commit message. Or, you can use -m and a message, which lets you specify the entire message just like git commit.

Git tries to figure out how to merge all the changes, but sometimes it can't. This is called a *conflict* and requires your intervention. Task 24, *Handling Conflicts*, on page 74 shows you how to handle these cases.

➤ Merge changes from development to the master branch.

```
prompt> git checkout master
Switched to branch 'master'
prompt> git merge development
Updating af0fe21..290b0d2
Fast-forward
 old/README.rst |    8 ++------
 1 files changed, 2 insertions(+), 6 deletions(-)
```

➤ Merge changes, but don't commit.

```
prompt> git merge --no-commit development
Automatic merge went well; stopped before committing...
```

➤ Force the creation of a merge commit.

```
prompt> git merge --no-ff development
Merge made by recursive.
 old/README.rst |    8 ++------
 1 files changed, 2 insertions(+), 6 deletions(-)
```

➤ Add a one-line log message from each merged commit to the merge message.

```
prompt> git merge --log development
```

➤ Specify a custom log message for a merge commit, if created.

```
prompt> git merge -m "my message" development
```

You can use git commit --amend to modify the commit message after the fact too. Here's an example:

```
prompt> git merge --log --no-ff development
prompt> git commit --amend -c HEAD
... editor launches ...
```

Related Tasks:

16   Rewriting History by Rebasing

Rebasing commits is the one concept in Git that has no counterpart inside the traditional version control world. Using git rebase, you can rewrite the history of a repository in a variety of ways. It is one of the most powerful commands in Git, which makes it one of the most dangerous.

rebase takes a series of commits (normally a branch) and replays them on top of another commit (normally the last commit in another branch). The parent commit changes so all the commit IDs are recalculated. This can cause problems for other developers who have your code because the IDs don't match up.

There's a simple rule of thumb with git rebase: use it as much as you want on local commits. Once you've shared changes with another developer, the headache is generally not worth the trouble.

git rebase takes a branch (the most common use), a tag, or a commit ID to rebase on top of. You can also pass the --rebase option to git pull, causing it to perform a rebase instead of merging the upstream changes into your local branch.

git rebase requires a clean working tree—that is, a working tree with no modified files. If you have changes that you're not ready to commit, you can stash them (see Task 26, *Temporarily Hiding Changes*, on page 78) until you're done.

A conflict might arise during the replaying of commits. Like a conflict during a regular merge, a conflict happens when two commits modify the same line of code. git rebase stops when this happens and asks you to fix the conflict (see Task 24, *Handling Conflicts*, on page 74) and then continue. You tell Git you're ready with git rebase --continue.

You can also skip a commit that's causing a conflict by calling git rebase --skip. That could lead to further conflicts, however. You can abort the rebase too with git rebase --abort.

There's always a safety net if you need to undo a rebase after it's completed. Git points ORIG_HEAD at the commit before major changes like git rebase are run. You can use git reset to reset your repository back to that original state.

➤ Rebase your current branch against another.

For example, rebase your current branch against master:

```
prompt> git rebase master
First, rewinding head to replay your work on top of it...
Applying: simple commit
```

You can also rebase against a tag or commit ID. For example, if af0fe21 is the commit ID for master, use this:

```
prompt> git rebase af0fe21
... same as above ...
```

➤ Undo a rebase after it completes.

```
prompt> git reset --hard ORIG_HEAD
HEAD is now at e9f9fdc update the README
```

Using --hard can be dangerous. Check Task 37, *Resetting Staged Changes and Commits*, on page 110 for an explanation of its use.

Before a Rebase

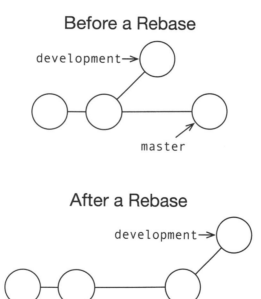

After a Rebase

Related Tasks:

- Task 15, *Merging Commits Between Branches*, on page 46
- Task 24, *Handling Conflicts*, on page 74
- Task 26, *Temporarily Hiding Changes*, on page 78
- Task 37, *Resetting Staged Changes and Commits*, on page 110

17   Deleting Branches

Branches can, and normally do, outlive their usefulness. Once you no longer need one, you can delete it from your repository. Remember, branches in Git are pointers to a commit. Deleting a branch doesn't delete any commits, just the named pointer that refers to that commit.

One area where Git differs from traditional version control systems is the expense related to creating and deleting branches. It's common to leave branches such as a release branch in the repository indefinitely in Subversion. Git doesn't require that.

Since tags and branches both point to a single commit, you can tag your release and then delete the release branch. You can always create a new branch from the tag later if you need to make a change and then retag the new version, and the history will look like the branch had always been there.

You can delete a branch with git branch -d. You must provide the branch name you want to delete. Git warns you if the branch you are trying to delete has not been merged into the current branch.

You can override this behavior by using -D (capital D). This tells Git that you want to delete the branch even if it hasn't been merged in.

➤ Delete a branch that has been merged into the current branch.

To delete a branch called experiment, do this:

```
prompt> git branch -d experiment
Deleted branch experiment (was e9f9fdc).
```

➤ Delete a branch that hasn't been merged into the current branch.

```
prompt> git branch -D experiment
Deleted branch experiment (was e9f9fdc).
```

Related Tasks:

- Task 18, *Tagging Milestones*, on page 52

18   Tagging Milestones

You need to make milestones in your projects, each slightly different, such as for one, its weekly iterations, and for another, its version numbers. You can use git tag to handle this.

git tag creates a read-only marker within the repository. You can treat tags like branch names, except you can't check them out and start committing to them. You can create a new branch from a tag, however.

Creating a tag requires one parameter: the name of the tag. Nearly every character you can use as part of a filename on Unix systems can be used as part of a tag name. You cannot use the characters ^, *, or :, and a tag cannot begin or end with /.

You can create a tag from a commit other than HEAD by supplying a second parameter to git tag. It can be a reference commit (either directly or relative to another commit) or a branch name (directly or relative as well).

Call git tag without any parameters to list all tags. One key difference between tags and branches is that there is no difference between a remote tag and a local tag. A tag is a tag.

➤ List all tags.

```
prompt> git tag
v0.1
v0.2
```

➤ Tag the latest commit as version 1.0 in the current branch.

```
prompt> git tag v1.0
prompt>
```

➤ Create a tag called beta1 from the next to last commit.

```
prompt> git tag beta1 HEAD^
prompt>
```

Related Tasks:

- Task 23, *Handling Remote Tags and Branches*, on page 68

Part IV

Working with a Team

Everything we've covered up to this point is about working with Git on your own. You can use Git like this to track your own projects, but that doesn't take full advantage of Git's power. You need to be able to collaborate with other developers on your team using Git.

You share code with other developers using *remote repositories*. Remote repositories are given names to make them easier to remember. For example, the conventional name for your default remote repository is origin.

There are two different ways to share code through a remote repository in Git: with a *shared repository model* or a *distributed repository model*. For a visual of these two models, see the following image of a shared and distributed repository layout with three developers. (Gray circles are the private repositories; outlined circles are public repositories.)

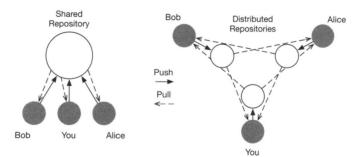

The one most familiar to those coming from another VCS is the *shared repository model*.

A shared repository means that all members of your team can push and pull from the same repository. Team members keep their changes locally until they're ready; then they push those changes back upstream when they're complete for the rest of the team to use.

This model is very familiar to anyone used to working with a traditional version control system. There's very little overhead in determining where the code is and what state everything is in.

You can also use a distributed repository model for handling your repositories. Each member of your team has their own private repositories on their computers plus a public repository that they push their code to. Each team member needs to pull changes from the other team members to make sure they have the latest code.

Most teams using a distributed model designate someone as the release manager. It becomes their job to make sure that everything is merged together, and that member's public repository becomes the repository of record. This is also common in open source projects using Git.

Many teams see the most benefit from a hybrid of these two approaches. One repository is considered the repository of record that everyone syncs against, and then developers share their changes through their public repositories. Once changes are ready to become part of the official version, they get pushed to the official repository.

In addition to the concept of remotes, these tasks introduce two new concepts you use to retrieve and send changes to remote repositories:

- *Fetching*, or retrieving changes from a remote repository, covered in Task 20, *Retrieving Remote Changes*, on page 62

- *Pushing*, or sending changes to a remote repository, discussed in Task 22, *Sending Changes to Remotes*, on page 66

You might wonder where *pulling* fits into this. The only difference between a pull (see Task 21, *Retrieving Remote Changes, Part II*, on page 64) and a fetch (see Task 20, *Retrieving Remote Changes*, on page 62) is that pulling merges changes after Git fetches them. It's a shorthand way to combine fetching and merging into one command.

All of these changes being retrieved from remote repositories are stored inside your local repository in *remote branches*. Git treats remote repositories—often called just *remotes*—as branches. All of the commits from the remotes are stored alongside your commits in the repository, and special remote branches track which commits have branches pointing to them.

You can treat remote branches like normal branches with one exception: you can't commit to them. That means you can merge or cherry-pick commits from them into your local branches or rebase your local branches on top of remote branches. The only way to get commits into a remote branch is to push those changes to the remote.

Covered in this part:

- First you need to know how to handle remote repositories. You learn that in Task 19, *Adding and Removing Remotes*, on page 60.

- Next up is fetching changes from remote repositories, which you learn about in Task 20, *Retrieving Remote Changes*, on page 62.

- After you know how to fetch changes, we go over the shorthand command for fetching and merging changes at the same time in Task 21, *Retrieving Remote Changes, Part II*, on page 64.

- Grabbing changes from other developers is only half the process. You need to be able to send your changes back out into the world. Task 22, *Sending Changes to Remotes*, on page 66 shows you how.

- We've already talked about tags and branches locally. You learn about remote tags in Task 23, *Handling Remote Tags and Branches*, on page 68.

Before you start concerning yourself with pushing and pulling, however, you need to add a remote repository to communicate with. Let's cover that next.

19   Adding and Removing Remotes

Git allows you to have as many remote repositories as you like. It's common to have a different remote for each member of your team in a fully distributed architecture for your repositories. Git requires that each remote have a unique name.

You must tell Git where to access remote repositories. You do this using the git remote add command.[15] It requires two parameters: a name and a repository URL.

The first is simply the short name you use to reference the remote repository by. The name origin is the conventional name for the repository that you clone from. Git uses this convention in several commands that allow you to skip the remote name when you're working with the origin repository.

The repository URL points to the actual location of the remote repository. This can be in another directory on your system or, more commonly, a repository that is accessible via a network connection. Git can transfer over its own git protocol, over git using SSH to encrypt the data transfer and handle authentication, and over HTTP/HTTPS.

Git sets up tracking branches for you whenever you create a local branch from a remote branch. Adding a repository after you start working locally, though, doesn't give Git a chance to do that setup. You can add this by removing the local branch and re-creating it from the remote branch. Don't worry—as long as you make sure all the changes in your local branch have been pushed to your remote repository and your local and remote branch have the same things in them, you aren't going to lose any commits.

You can remove remote repositories by using the git remote rm command. It removes any tracking branch information in addition to removing the remote definition.

---

15. Most commands that require a remote repository take both remote names —what you add with git remote add—or the repository URL.

➤ Add a new remote repository.

```
prompt> git remote add <name> <repository URL>
... example ...
prompt> git remote add tswicegood \
    git://github.com/tswicegood/bobby-tables.git
propmt>
```

➤ Remove a remote.

```
prompt> git remote rm <name>
... example ...
prompt> git remote rm tswicegood
```

➤ Make the master branch a tracking branch.

Run these commands after you push to your remote repository for the first time if you want to set up your local branch as a tracking branch of the remote. As an example, here's the workflow in a project of mine:

```
prompt> git checkout origin/master
Note: checking out 'origin/master'.

You are in 'detached HEAD' state. ... and so on ...

  git checkout -b new_branch_name

HEAD is now at d7c8880... ignore stuff from virtualenv
prompt> git branch -d master
Deleted branch master (was d7c8880).
prompt> git checkout -b master
Switched to a new branch 'master'
```

Related Tasks:

- Task 4, *Creating a Local Copy of an Existing Repository,* on page 10
- Task 13, *Creating and Switching Branches,* on page 42
- Task 20, *Retrieving Remote Changes,* on page 62
- Task 21, *Retrieving Remote Changes, Part II,* on page 64
- Task 22, *Sending Changes to Remotes,* on page 66

20   Retrieving Remote Changes

You must keep your repository in sync with the changes from everyone else that is collaborating on it with you. You do this with the git fetch command. Fetching is closely related to git pull, and many people incorrectly use the two commands interchangeably.

Fetching changes from a remote repository retrieves—literally fetches —the changes from that remote repository. This stores them in their remote branches on your local repository. You can use this to see what changes are on the remote repository without affecting your local repository.

Git fetches the changes from the origin remote repository if you don't specify a remote. You can fetch from another repository by providing the name of that remote repository. By default, it fetches all branches from a remote repository. You can change this depending on the parameters you provide to git fetch.

You can fetch a specific branch by calling git fetch with an explicit remote name and a refspec. Refspecs provide the name of the remote branch and the branch in your local repository that it should be fetched into separated by a colon. For example, to fetch only the master branch from your origin branch, you use this: git fetch origin master:remotes/origin/master.

This format might look a little wonky at first glance. Most of the time you refer to a remote branch by <remote name>/<branch name> without the remotes/ prefix. Its full name contains the remotes/ prefix, however, and you must use its full name with this command.

You can fetch changes from multiple remotes at one time. You can use the --multiple parameter to provide Git with multiple remotes to fetch changes from. Use --all to tell Git to go through all of your remotes and fetch the changes from them.

➤ Fetch changes from remote repository.

```
prompt> git fetch <remote name>
... example ...
prompt> git fetch tswicegood
remote: Counting objects: 39, done.
remote: Compressing objects: 100% (25/25), done.
remote: Total 39 (delta 16), reused 26 (delta 9)
Unpacking objects: 100% (39/39), done.
From git://github.com/tswicegood/bobby-tables
 * [new branch]      master     -> tswicegood/master
```

➤ Fetch a specific branch.

This requires a peculiar refspec to make sure the fetched branch ends up in the right place in your local repository.

```
prompt> git fetch remote  \
       local branch:remotes/remote/remote branch
```

To fetch master from origin to your local copy of the origin/master remote branch, use this:

```
prompt> git fetch origin master:remotes/origin/master
```

➤ Fetch changes from multiple remote repositories.

```
prompt> git fetch --multiple remote1  remote2 ... and so on ...
```

➤ Fetch changes from all remote repositories.

```
prompt> git fetch --all
... example after adding another remote ...
prompt> git fetch --all
Fetching tswicegood
Fetching petdance
remote: Counting objects: 414, done.
remote: Compressing objects: 100% (161/161), done.
remote: Total 407 (delta 231), reused 397 (delta 227)
Receiving objects: 100% (407/407), 52.53 KiB, done.
Resolving deltas: 100% (231/231), completed with 2 local objects.
From http://github.com/petdance/bobby-tables
 * [new branch]      master     -> petdance/master
```

Related Tasks:

21   Retrieving Remote Changes, Part II

Many people new to Git treat git fetch and git pull as synonyms. Understanding the differences between the two is important to understanding how Git handles remote repositories. Remember, remotes are read-only branches. You fetch changes from a remote repository into those branches (which are stored locally), instead of committing directly to them, and then merge those changes as necessary. You can use git pull to combine fetching and merging into one command.

git pull follows Git's convention and assumes that you want to pull from the origin remote repository if you do not specify a remote. You must specify a remote if you want to provide a specific branch to pull from.

You can provide a full refspec—two branches separated by a colon— to control which branch you are pulling from and which branch you want those changes to end up in. You specify the remote branch before the colon and the local branch after the colon. You can pull into branches that don't exist.

You can use the --rebase option to tell Git to rebase your local changes on top of the remote changes instead of performing a merge. This is the equivalent of running git fetch followed by git rebase. This allows you to cleanly apply all your local changes on top of the remote changes that have already been shared.

➤ Pull changes from a remote repository.

```
prompt> git pull [name [branch name]]
... example ...
prompt> git pull tswicegood master
From git://github.com/tswicegood/bobby-tables
 * branch              master      -> FETCH_HEAD
```

➤ Pull changes from a different branch into your local branch.

```
prompt> git pull origin <remote branch>:<local branch>
... example ...
prompt> git pull origin development:team-dev
```

➤ Pull changes and rebase instead of merge.

To fetch from origin and rebase against its main branch, use this:

```
prompt> git pull --rebase origin master
From git://github.com/origin/bobby-tables
 * branch              master      -> FETCH_HEAD
First, rewinding head to replay your work on top of it...
Applying: add <meta> tags
```

Related Tasks:

22   Sending Changes to Remotes

You have to publish your repository somewhere that is accessible to other members of your team. You send your changes to that repository using the git push command.

Calling git push without any parameters causes Git to assume you want to push all of your local branches that have a matching branch on the origin repository. You can provide both a remote repository and a branch name.

git push takes both named remote repositories (that is, those that have been added via git remote add) and full URLs to remote repositories.

You can provide a branch name to specify which branch to push, but in order to provide a branch, you must specify a remote repository. For example, to push your beta branch to your origin repository, you would use this: git push origin beta.

You can also use the more verbose refspec syntax if you want to push to a remote branch that is named differently than your local branch. The syntax of a refspec for git push is two branches separated by a colon — the local branch first followed by the name of the remote branch. For example, pushing your local master branch to a remote branch named beta, you use this: git push origin master:beta.

Git attempts to keep you from updating a repository in a way that could cause issues for others who have cloned your repository. By default, it does not allow you to push non-fast-forward changes to a remote repository (see introduction to Part III, *Organizing Your Repository with Branches and Tags*, for more information on types of merges).

Non-fast-forward merges are generally caused by one of two things: 1) someone else has pushed changes to the remote repository; or 2) you've made a modification to your local repository history. For the first case, fetch the remote changes, and then merge them into your local branch (via git rebase or git merge). The second case could be caused by a rebase, amending commits, or resetting the repository.

You normally don't want to update a remote repository without using a fast-forward push, but in those rare cases where it is necessary or desired (you committed sensitive information or are removing a commit that does not need to be recorded, for example), you can use the --force or -f option to force Git to allow the update.

➤ Push the local tracking branch to your origin.

prompt> `git push`

➤ Push first set of changes from master to your origin.

prompt> `git push origin master`

➤ Push changes from a specific branch to a specific remote repository.

```
prompt> git push <remote name>  <branch name>
... example ...
prompt> git push tswicegood development
Counting objects: 42, done.
Delta compression using up to 2 threads.
Compressing objects: 100% (33/33), done.
Writing objects: 100% (42/42), 39.49 KiB, done.
Total 42 (delta 18), reused 5 (delta 4)
Unpacking objects: 100% (42/42), done.
To git://internal.domain51.pvt/sample-repo.git
 * [new branch]      development -> development
```

For example, to push to the production branch to the shared remote, use this:

prompt> `git push shared production`

➤ Push changes from the local master branch to the remote production branch.

prompt> `git push origin master:production`

➤ Force a remote branch to accept a push.

Warning: Use this with extreme caution because it can cause others to get out of sync with the repository to which you are pushing.

```
prompt> git push --force
... or ...
prompt> git push -f
```

Related Tasks:

- Task 4, *Creating a Local Copy of an Existing Repository*, on page 10
- Task 15, *Merging Commits Between Branches*, on page 46
- Task 19, *Adding and Removing Remotes*, on page 60
- Task 21, *Retrieving Remote Changes, Part II*, on page 64

| 23 | Handling Remote Tags and Branches |

You can push your tags to a remote repository by one of two mechanisms: you can call git push and supply the tag name as the reference to push, or you can add the --tags parameter to git push to push all your tags to the remote.

Most tags are fetched automatically. Fetching changes from master that has several tags in its history causes Git to fetch those tags as well. Like git push --tags, you can explicitly fetch tags via git fetch --tags.

Be careful with tags, however. Remote tags always win when there are two tags with the same name. For example, consider if your repository has a v1.0 tag that points to a specific commit, and your remote repository has a v1.0 tag that points to a different commit. When you pull changes from that remote, your v1.0 tag is going to change to reflect the latest.

The best way to handle this is through procedure. Determine who is responsible on your team for tagging commits and the way you're going to name tags,[16] and stick to it.

You have to explicitly push a branch to get a local branch to show up on a remote repository. Likewise, you have to explicitly delete remote branches to remove them.

You can delete remote branches with a special-case refspec and git push :<branch to delete>. This is the equivalent of pushing an empty branch to the remote repository.

---

16. Semantic Versioning (http://semver.org/) is a great place to start.

➤ Push tag v1.0 to the origin.

```
prompt> git push origin v1.0
Total 0 (delta 0), reused 0 (delta 0)
To git://internal.domain51.pvt/sample-repo.git
 * [new tag]         v1.0 -> v1.0
```

➤ Push all tags to the origin.

```
prompt> git push --tags origin
Total 0 (delta 0), reused 0 (delta 0)
To git://internal.domain51.pvt/sample-repo.git
 * [new tag]         v0.8 -> v0.8
 * [new tag]         v0.9 -> v0.9
```

➤ Fetch remote tags and update local tags.

```
prompt> git fetch --tags origin
remote: Counting objects: 42, done.
remote: Compressing objects: 100% (37/37), done.
remote: Total 42 (delta 18), reused 0 (delta 0)
Unpacking objects: 100% (42/42), done.
From git://internal.domain51.pvt/sample-repo.git
 * [new tag]         v0.8        -> v0.8
 * [new tag]         v0.9        -> v0.9
 * [new tag]         v1.0        -> v1.0
```

➤ Delete the remote branch called beta.

```
prompt> git push origin :beta
From git://internal.domain51.pvt/sample-repo.git
 - [deleted]         beta
```

Related Tasks:

• Task 18, *Tagging Milestones,* on page 52

Part V

Branches and Merging Revisited

Now you have the basics down, understand the concepts of branches, and have the know-how to collaborate with other developers. It's time to revisit branches and some of the more advanced things you can do with them.

For basic branch usage, see Part III, *Organizing Your Repository with Branches and Tags*. This part covers tasks related to managing branches once they've been created. For example, what happens when you edit the same file in different ways in two branches and then attempt to merge them back together? A conflict can occur. We cover multiple ways to handle that in this part.

Covered in this part:

- Conflicts are going to happen. Git tries to figure out how to handle merging changes as best it can, but sometimes it can't. Task 24, *Handling Conflicts*, on page 74, covers how to fix cases where a conflict is created.

- You can also use a GUI tool for managing conflicts. Task 25, *Handling Conflicts with a GUI*, on page 76, covers that.

- Sometimes you need to temporarily hide changes in your working tree. We see how you do this in Task 26, *Temporarily Hiding Changes*, on page 78.

- There's more than one way to get changes between branches. Task 27, *Cherry-Picking Commits*, on page 80, introduces you to another way to pull individual changes from one branch into another.

- We revisit the git rebase command in Task 28, *Controlling How You Replay Commits*, on page 82, to learn how to use rebase interactively.

- You can move branches around. There are several ways to do this, depending on the circumstance. Look at Task 29, *Moving Branches*, on page 84, to see how.

Now, let's brush up on our conflict resolution skills.

24   Handling Conflicts

You can't develop a project with other developers without generating conflicting versions of code from time to time. Git goes a long way toward helping you resolve those automatically, but sometimes it can't.

For example, the code shown on the opposite page shows two different solutions to the same problem. You must tell Git how to fix the conflict because it doesn't know which version is correct. They both make changes to the exact same lines of code. You can find out which file or files have conflicts in two ways: the output from the failed git merge, or git status.

You can find conflicts within a file by looking for <<<<<<< —seven lesser than signs—with a commit such as HEAD. The original code— the code inside the branch you're merging into—is located between the 7 < and ========. The new code is between that marker and >>>>>>>, followed by the name of branch (or commit ID, tag, and so on) you were merging in.

How you deal with the conflict and determine which version to use is up to you. You can choose one version over the other, use one and then the other, combine the two changes together, or completely remove them both.

Once you've resolved the conflict, call git add to stage the new changes and then git commit to commit it. You might not have anything to commit, however. For example, if you use all the changes from your local branch, Git doesn't need to create a new commit. Nothing has changed.

You can also abort a conflict at any time before you commit the changes by resetting your working tree to ORIG_HEAD. See Task 37, *Resetting Staged Changes and Commits,* on page 110 for more about git reset.

Here's an example of how a conflict can happen between two branches:

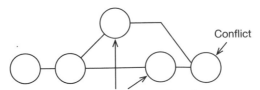

Both commits change the same line of code

➤ See an example merge conflict.

The basics of the error message are the same, but the files are always different. For example, here's a conflict in a repository for one of my projects:

```
prompt> git merge added_raw
Auto-merging dolt.py
CONFLICT (content): Merge conflict in dolt.py
Automatic merge failed; fix conflicts and then commit the result.
```

You can find the conflict inside the file by looking for the special markup that Git adds, <<<<<<< followed by a commit (most of the time HEAD. Here's the conflict in the previous file:

```
<<<<<<< HEAD
    def _handle_response(self, response, data=[], raw=False):
        return data if raw else simplejson.loads(data)
=======
    def _handle_response(self, response, raw=False, data=[]):
        if raw:
            return data
        return simplejson.loads(data)
>>>>>>> added_raw
```

➤ Commit a fixed conflict.

You can use git status to see whether the conflict still exists:

```
# On branch master
# Unmerged paths:
#   (use "git add/rm <file>..." as appropriate to mark resolution)
#
#       both modified:      dolt.py
#
```

Once the conflict is resolved, call git add and git commit like you normally would.

Related Tasks:

25   Handling Conflicts with a GUI

Merging is often made easier with a GUI that displays each version of the code in question and allows you to choose which version you prefer. You can use git mergetool to launch a GUI tool to handle merge conflicts.

You can choose from several different merge tools. Their availability varies between platforms, and how you interact with a tool is slightly different for each one you use for merging. Generally, the local copy (the original that was in your branch before the merge) is displayed on the left, with the remote, new code on the right.

Common to all GUI merge tools is the ability to step through each change and choose which version you like. You must save those changes before exiting. git mergetool looks at the result and stages that as the correct version of the conflicting code.

You have to commit your changes once the conflict has been resolved, just like manually merging the conflicts (see Task 24, *Handling Conflicts*, on page 74). git mergetool stages the changes for you; that's the only difference.

➤ Launch a merge tool to handle a conflict.

```
prompt> git mergetool
merge tool candidates: opendiff kdiff3 tkdiff xxdiff meld
    tortoisemerge gvimdiff diffuse ecmerge p4merge araxis emerge vimdiff
Merging the files: dolt.py

Normal merge conflict for 'dolt.py':
  {local}: modified
  {remote}: modified
Hit return to start merge resolution tool (opendiff):
```

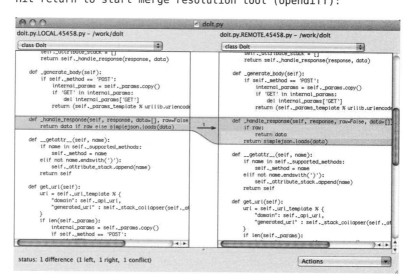

➤ Set gvimdiff as the default merge tool.

```
prompt> git config --global merge.tool "gvimdiff"
```

➤ Use the Perforce Visual Merge Tool[17] on Windows.

This example shows the Window-specific command, but you can use the same process on any platform for a custom merge tool.

```
prompt> git config --global merge.tool p4merge
prompt> git config --global mergetool.p4merge.cmd \
    'p4merge.exe \"$BASE\" \"$LOCAL\" \"$REMOTE\" \"$MERGED\"'
```

Related Tasks:

---

17. http://www.perforce.com/perforce/products/merge.html

26 Temporarily Hiding Changes

Some Git operations, such as git rebase, require a clean working tree—a working tree with no changes. git stash gives you a tool to hide changes that aren't quite ready to commit so you can come back to them.

Stashing changes is the equivalent of creating a commit and then resetting your repository back one commit. Stash provides a mechanism for grabbing those changes out of history more easily, however.

Stash names are similar to the names you see in the reflog (see Task 40, *Retrieving "Lost" Commits*, on page 116). You refer to them as stash@{#}, replacing the # with the age of the stash. The most recent is 0, the one before that is 1, and so on.

You can call git stash without any parameters to create a new stash. Calling it without any parameters is the same as calling it with git stash save. Providing the save option allows you to specify a message explaining what the stash was.

There are two commands to apply previous stashes to your current working tree: apply and pop. You can use apply to make the change to your working tree without removing the stashed change from your stash. Most of the time, you want to apply it and remove it from the stash, though. That's where pop comes in. It "pops" the change off the stack and applies it.

Creating stashes stores the commits outside of normal branches. To see what stashed changes are available, you can use the git stash list command. Like the name hints at, it lists all the stashed changes.

You can use the --patch parameter to stash a portion of the change. It works just like git add -p (see Task 6, *Staging Changes to Commit*, on page 20).

Sometimes you create a stash and then realize you don't need it any longer. You can use git stash drop <stash name> to delete an individual stash, or you can use the clear option to remove all the stashed changes.

Another interesting use of git stash is the branch option. You can use it to create a new branch from a stash. Git creates a new branch for you that looks exactly like your repository did when you called git stash originally. This is useful for applying a stash to see its changes in situations where the stash does not apply cleanly to the current working tree.

➤ Stash the changes in your working tree.

```
prompt> git stash
Saved working directory and index state WIP on
    master: 8e323b6 add <meta> tags
HEAD is now at 8e323b6 add <meta> tags
```

➤ Apply a stash to the current working tree.

```
prompt> git stash apply
... output looks similar to git status after apply ...
```

Or, to apply and remove from the stash, use this:

```
prompt> git stash pop
... same output as above plus ...
Dropped refs/stash@{0} (76d9092...)
```

➤ List the available stashes.

```
prompt> git stash list
stash@{0}: WIP on master: 8e323b6 add <meta> tags
```

➤ Create a stash in patch mode.

```
prompt> git stash save --patch
... launches editor ...
```

➤ Delete stashes.

```
prompt> git stash drop <stash name>
Dropped stash@{0} (ea5bd0c...)
```

Or, to remove all stashed changes, use this:

```
prompt> git stash clear
prompt>
```

➤ Create a branch from an existing stash.

```
prompt> git stash branch <branch name> [<stash name>]
```

Related Tasks:

27   Cherry-Picking Commits

You sometimes need to grab one commit from another branch and merge it into your local branch, such as a bug fix that needs to be backported. You can grab commits one at a time using git cherry-pick.

Cherry-picking a commit from another takes that single commit and commits it to your local branch. It's pretty straightforward and appears extremely useful in a lot of situations, but be careful.

Cherry-picked commits have different commit IDs than the original commit they came from because their parent changed—remember that a commit ID is based partially on where it exists in the history, and changing the parent changes the commit ID. A good rule of thumb is to cherry-pick commits only when a merge is not an option, in other words, backporting a bug fix where the backported change is never going to be merged forward.

You must specify the commit that you want to cherry-pick. You can do this with either a commit ID, a branch name, a tag, or some relative reference to any of these. Keep in mind that using a branch name or tag means that the latest commit that those reference is cherry-picked in, not the entire history.

Normally git cherry-pick automatically creates a new commit as soon as it is done. You can change this behavior with two different options. Use --edit (or -e) to launch the editor and change the commit message before committing the cherry-picked revision. This allows you to edit the commit message but not the actual commit.

You can use --no-commit (or -n) to tell Git to stop as soon as the change has been merged and staged. You can use this to cherry-pick several commits and then commit them into your local branch as one commit. Remember to start with the oldest commit first when cherry-picking more than one commit; otherwise, you might end up trying to make a change that isn't possible or having conflicts because it is in the wrong order.

You can also add a Signed-off-by line to the end of a cherry-picked commit. Signed-off lines consist of the phrase Signed-off-by: followed by your name and email address (pulled from the configuration). This is useful for creating a chain of review for commits and can become essential in backported commits to ensure they have been properly reviewed prior to being merged into an existing branch.

➤ Merge a single commit from another branch into your local one.

prompt> `git cherry-pick some commit ID`

some commit ID refers to a commit any way you normally can: an actual
commit ID, branch name, tag, or some relative version of any of those.
For example, to cherry-pick the latest from release_1.0 or commit
a74cc83, use this:

```
prompt> git cherry-pick release_1.0
Finished one cherry-pick.
[master bcdbca8] add <meta> tags
 1 files changed, 1 insertions(+), 0 deletions(-)
prompt> git cherry-pick a74cc83
Finished one cherry-pick.
[master dd94f18] working on conerting to Textile
 Author: Andy Lester <andy@petdance.com>
 5 files changed, 195 insertions(+), 176 deletions(-)
 rewrite crank (81%)
 create mode 100644 s/index.textile
 create mode 100644 s/java.textile
```

➤ Cherry-pick, but edit the commit message before committing.

```
prompt> git cherry-pick --edit release_1.0
... or ...
prompt> git cherry-pick -e release_1.0
```

➤ Cherry-pick, but don't commit.

```
prompt> git cherry-pick --no-commit release_1.0
... or ...
prompt> git cherry-pick -n release_1.0
```

➤ Add a "Signed-off-by" line to the commit message.

```
prompt> git cherry-pick --signoff release_1.0
... or ...
prompt> git cherry-pick -s release_1.0
```

Related Tasks:

• Task 7, *Committing Changes*, on page 22
• Task 15, *Merging Commits Between Branches*, on page 46

28   Controlling How You Replay Commits

Rebasing in Git replays one set of commits on top of another. We covered the basic case in Task 16, *Rewriting History by Rebasing*, on page 48. There is an interactive mode to git rebase that lets you control how the commits are replayed.

Like a regular rebase, git rebase -i takes the commits in your current branch and replays them against another point in your repository's history. You can use this to change the order of commits, squash commits together, or edit a previous commit. Consider the following example.

You add a new feature and then start working on the next feature. You realize a little while later that you could have implemented it in a cleaner fashion. You could amend the commit (see Task 35, *Fixing Commits*, on page 106) if it's the last commit, but since some time has elapsed, you've already created other commits.

This is where interactive rebasing comes into play. Create the second commit with the fix you want to use, and then launch git rebase -i and pass it the commit ID of the original commit ID minus one. For example, if the commit ID was 322dafc, you should use git rebase -i 322dafc^.

Git rebase's interactive mode launches your editor with a list of commits. You can use the editor to move the last line (the commit you just made) up to immediately after the commit you want to merge it into; then change the first word to say fixup to merge it into the original commit.

There five different options: pick, reword, edit, squash, and fixup. You can use any of these as the first word or the first letter of a line to adjust that commit when it is replayed.

Like a regular git rebase, be careful how you rebase. You can cause issues for other people who have synced off of your repository if you rebase code that you've already shared. Remember this simple rule of thumb: don't rebase code you've shared.

➤ Rebase interactively.

```
prompt> git rebase -i <commit ID
... example ...
prompt> git rebase -i HEAD~5
```

For example, to interactively rebase the last five commits, use this:

```
prompt> git rebase -i HEAD~5
... or ...
prompt> git rebase -i HEAD^^^^^
```

➤ See an example interactive rebase.

The following is the result of a git rebase -i on one of my projects:

```
pick 6b24857 remove theme from repo
pick 29e2376 add in dependency on external repo for theme
pick 7ce4bdf add code to handle deployment of new docs

# Rebase 86968d5..7ce4bdf onto 86968d5
#
# Commands:
#  p, pick = use commit
#  r, reword = use commit, but edit the commit message
#  e, edit = use commit, but stop for amending
#  s, squash = use commit, but meld into previous commit
#  f, fixup = like "squash", but discard this commit's log message
#
# If you remove a line here THAT COMMIT WILL BE LOST.
# However, if you remove everything, the rebase will be aborted.
#
```

Related Tasks:

- Task 15, *Merging Commits Between Branches*, on page 46
- Task 16, *Rewriting History by Rebasing*, on page 48

29   Moving Branches

Sometimes you need to move branches around to reorganize them. For example, you have a branch where you're working on a future version of your software. During the rewrite, your team realizes that the better-widget feature can be released as a minor version of your software instead of being part of the next major version. This is where you can move a branch to make your repository more sane.

You use git rebase --onto to move branches. Like a normal git rebase, Git replays the commits from one branch against another. The difference is that Git takes the branch you're rebasing, and instead of replaying it against another branch, it moves it to an entirely different one.

The syntax is more verbose than a simple git rebase that requires only one additional parameter. git rebase --onto takes three: the first is the branch you're rebasing onto, the second is the branch you're rebasing from, and the third is the branch you want to move.

➤ Move branch better-widget from next-release to master.

This is the current state of the repository: the next-release branch was created from the master branch, and the better-widget branch was created from the next-release branch.

```
o--master--o
            \
             o--next-release--o
                               \
                                o--better-widget--o
```

The command to move the branch is a specialized version of git rebase:

prompt> **git rebase --onto master next-release better-widget**

After running this command, use this:

```
             o--better-widget--o
            /
o--master--o
            \
             o--next-release--o
```

next-release is moved to the end of master, so if there were more commits in master than were in next-release, better-widget is placed on top of those. Here's an example:

```
o--master--o--o--o
            \
             o--next-release--o
                               \
                                o--better-widget--o
```

After running git rebase --onto, use this:

```
                o--better-widget--o
               /
o--master--o--o--o
            \
             o--next-release--o
```

Related Tasks:

• Task 16, *Rewriting History by Rebasing,* on page 48

Part VI

Working with the Repository's History

You've learned all the basics, as well as some of the more complex topics in Git. It's time to start looking at all that history you've been building up and put the code in the context it was created in.

Your repository is a vault of all the changes you and your team have made to your project. Git tracks all of those changes and their commit messages, making them viewable and searchable via the *log*.

The log is a reverse chronological view of each commit. By default, it shows you the commit ID, the author, the committer (if that person is different from the author), the date, and the log message. You can show more (or less) in that output.

The power of Git's log feature is directly related to how your project handles commit messages. The more information you add to your commit message, the more valuable the log is to your developers.

Git convention for commit messages is to break the messages into two parts. Start with a one-line "subject" that tersely describes the change that was made, and then follow it with a more in-depth "body" that describes the change in plain text. The rule of thumb is to explain the change like you're explaining it to another developer. Let the code speak for itself, but make sure to include reasons for the change and explain any potentially odd choices.

Covered in this part:

- We start with the log in Task 30, *Viewing the Log*, on page 92. You'll learn how to view the log in a couple of different formats and how to understand the information it displays.

- Once you understand the basics of querying Git's log, Task 31, *Filtering the Log Output*, on page 94 walks you through filtering those results through Git's revisions and ranges.

- Each commit tracks changes between files. Those changes are described as *diffs*. You'll learn how to view Git's diffs in Task 32, *Comparing Differences*, on page 96 so you can see changes across different commits.

- Everyone loves statistics. Well, at least managers do. In addition to the excellent diffs and logs that Git provides, it also gives you the ability to generate some statistics on the changes your repository is tracking. You'll learn how to use these tools in Task 33, *Generating Statistics About Changes*, on page 98.

- Finally, we wrap up this part with a section on blame. The logs provide us with excellent information on individual changes. In Task 34, *Assigning Blame*, on page 100, you learn how inspect information about each line of a file. It's excellent for assigning blame—er, praise— on the other members of your team when you find their excellently unique code.

Now, let's jump into the basic display of your repository's history: the log.

30   Viewing the Log

Git's bread and butter is tracking changes to files in your project over a period of time. You use the log to view that history.

You can use git log to view the standard log output. Git displays the commit ID, author, date, and commit message for each commit in reverse chronological order. Git sends the output through less to keep the output from scrolling past on the screen too fast to be seen.

You can use the --oneline parameter to shorten the log display to show the first seven characters of the commit ID and the subject of the log message. It increases the number of commits you can view on one screen and with properly written log messages makes scanning easier.

Viewing the entire history often gives you too much information. You can limit the number of commits git log shows by providing it with -N, changing N with the number of commits you want to display.

Often you need to see the changes made to the file in addition to the log message to fully understand the change. You can use the -p to show the diff the commit made.

➤ View a reverse chronological list of all commits.

```
prompt> git log
commit 3ac20cfb09212f212a2f60a6227610c680e8a95e
Author: Travis Swicegood <development@domain51.com>
Date:   Wed Aug 18 09:29:38 2010 -0500

    add sample output for Part V


commit fa0016322bf4e73d1419ddc91777368db0f35484
Author: Travis Swicegood <development@domain51.com>
Date:   Wed Aug 18 09:12:35 2010 -0500

    add in sample output for Part IV

... and so on, and so on ...
```

➤ View the log with one shortened commit ID and subject.

```
prompt> git log --oneline
3ac20cf add sample output for Part V
fa00163 add in sample output for Part IV
8bd724b add note about empty prompt> to the intro
... and so on, and so on ...
```

➤ View the last N commits.

```
prompt> git log -N
... examples ...
prompt> git log -5                  # show the last five
prompt> git log HEAD^^^^^..HEAD # show the last five
prompt> git log -10                 # show the last ten
prompt> git log HEAD~10..HEAD   # show the last ten
```

➤ Show the changes made in the latest commit.

```
prompt> git log -1 -p HEAD
```

Note that it is a 1 (as in the number) and not an l (as in *library*).

Related Tasks:

• Task 32, *Comparing Differences,* on page 96

31   Filtering the Log Output

Git's log is useful way to track what the original developer—often yourself—was thinking when they made a change, but it often provides too much information. You can use git log's many parameters to filter the results it displays, zeroing in on the information that's important to you.

You can start to filter the results by providing Git with a directory or path. You specify the path as the last parameter. To be safe, separate the path from other parameters with -- (two dashes). Otherwise, Git can't tell the difference between the branch or tag work and the path work.

You can also filter the log based on the time of the commit. Using the --since or --after parameter, you can look at commits after a given point in time. Git attempts to parse any string you give it but fails silently if it can't parse the date you provide. Stick with traditional date and time formats or a number followed by months, weeks, days, hours, minutes, and so on, to make sure Git can understand you.

Git provides you with the opposite of --since and --after too; you can use --until or --before to look for commits older than a given time.

You use --author to filter the results by author or email address. Git matches on a partial name; --author="Travis" match both the commits I make and commits authored by "The Other Travis."

Finally, you can use --grep to search through the log messages using a regular expression, or *regexp*. It uses basic regular expressions, just like the command-line tool it takes its name from—grep. You can tell it to ignore case with the --regexp-ignore-case or the shorter -i parameters.

➤ Limit the log output to a single file or directory.

```
prompt> git log -- some/path/
prompt> git log -- some_file
```

➤ View the commits in the last week.

You can use many kinds of times with --since or --after. Here are a few variations of looking at the last week of commits:

```
prompt> git log --since="1 week"
... or ...
prompt> git log --after="7 days"
... or ...
prompt> git log --since="168 hours"
```

➤ View the commits prior to the last week.

```
prompt> git log --before="1 week"
... or ...
prompt> git log --until="7 days"
... or ...
prompt> git log --before="168 hours"
```

➤ View the log entries by a single committer.

```
prompt> git log --author="some user"
```

➤ View the log entries containing a regular expression.

```
prompt> git log --grep="some [Rr]eg[Ee]x"
... or ...
prompt> git log --grep="some regex" --regexp-ignore-case
... or ...
prompt> git log --grep="some regex" -i
```

Related Tasks:

- Task 30, *Viewing the Log*, on page 92

32	**Comparing Differences**

Git's log provides you with the information about a change—who made it, what their intent was, and so on—but sometimes looking at the changes made to the code provides more information. git diff shows you the changes that were made between two commits.

You can use git diff to view the changes—referred to as *diffs* or *patches* —of two different commits or states. Most of the time it's called as git diff with no parameters. That's the same as telling Git, "Show me the changes between my working tree and the staging area."

git diff considers changes that are staged and ready to be committed as part of the repository. You can tell Git to show the differences between what is staged and what is stored in the repository by adding the --staged parameter. Note that this output does not show any changes that are in your working tree but not yet staged.

You can also provide a single, explicit commit ID to git diff to tell Git to compare your current working tree against what is in the repository at that point. For example, if you want to compare your working tree against the latest commit, regardless of what has been staged, you can provide the HEAD parameter to tell Git to compare against that commit.

Most of the time you use git diff one of the ways discussed, but you can use it in other ways. For example, you can provide a first and second commit to compare the differences between those two commits.

Looking at the differences between two commits that are far apart might generate a lot more noise than you need. You can limit the files shown in the diff by providing a path. The best practice is to include the path after a --, which tells Git, "This is a path, not a revision." Without that, Git can confuse the path you provide with a branch or tag of the same name.

➤ View the differences between the current working tree and the staging area.

```
prompt> git diff
```

➤ View the differences between the staged changes and repository.

```
prompt> git diff --staged
```

➤ View the differences between the working tree and a commit in the repository.

```
prompt> git diff HEAD
prompt> git diff Commit ID
```

➤ View the differences between two "commits."

You can use a commit ID, branch name, or tag to reference a commit here.

```
prompt> git diff first  second
... or ...
prompt> git diff first..second
... example ...
prompt> git diff 423d021 1e85ac3
... or ...
prompt> git diff 423d021..1e85ac3
```

➤ Limit the diff output to a specific path.

```
prompt> git diff -- path/
```

Related Tasks:

- Task 5, *Seeing What Has Changed,* on page 18
- Task 30, *Viewing the Log,* on page 92
- Task 33, *Generating Statistics About Changes,* on page 98

33   Generating Statistics About Changes

The individual commit's changes are important, but viewing those changes in aggregate through statistics can provide you with a unique view of the project. Git helps you do that through the various statistical outputs it generates.

Git's git diff --stat is the most straightforward of the displays. It takes one or two commits—remember, git diff assumes HEAD as its second commit if you don't specify it—and displays stats regarding the changes rather than displaying the diff output. It includes file-by-file changes in addition to the summary statistics. Git uses the diffstat command for this, so the output may look familiar if you're used to that program.

Sometimes all you need is the final line of the stats output—the number of files changed, the number of insertions, and the number of deletions. Use --shortstat to display that information. It's the same information displayed at the last line of the main --stat output but without the file-by-file breakdown.

The output generated by the --stat and --shortstat parameters is not easily parseable by a computer. You can use the --numstat parameter to generate a three-column output that is easy to parse. The first column is the number of inserted lines, the second is the number of deleted lines, and the final column is the name of the file in question.

You can generate stats using any range of revisions that work with git diff. Adding any of the stat parameters tells Git to output the stats without showing the actual differences. Add -p to the command to show both the statistical output and patch or to show the differences.

We've talked about viewing statistical information in the context of git diff, but you can also view it from git log along with each log message. Add --stat, --shortstat, or --numstat to any git log command to add the respective statistical output to the log output.

➤ Show change stats between the last ten commits.

```
prompt> git diff --stat HEAD~10
... or ...
prompt> git diff --stat HEAD~10 HEAD
```

➤ Show statistics between two commits.

```
prompt> git diff --stat first  second
... example ...
prompt> git diff --stat 423d021 1e85ac3
```

➤ Show the number of files changed, inserts, and deletes in the last ten commits.

```
prompt> git diff --shortstat HEAD~10
```

➤ Show stats in a parseable format.

```
prompt> git diff --numstat HEAD~10
```

➤ Show the patch in addition to the statistical information.

```
prompt> git diff --stat -p HEAD^
```

➤ Show statistics about commits in the log.

For full stats by file:

```
prompt> git log --stat
```

To display cumulative stats only, use this:

```
prompt> git log --shortstat
```

Related Tasks:

34   Assigning Blame

Despite its combative name, git blame is a useful tool for determining what the original developer was thinking. Most bugs manifest themselves with an error at a specific point. You can use git blame to find out when the problem line was introduced into the repository and use that as a jumping-off point for further investigation.

git blame displays all or a portion of a file with annotations showing when the change was made, by who, and, more importantly, in what revision the change was made. Armed with that, you can inspect the log to determine what the original author intended.

git blame outputs the following information:

- Short commit ID
- Author's name
- Date and time of commit
- Line number

By default, the entire file is displayed. You can limit the portion of the file displayed by using the -L parameter. It requires one parameter: a number or POSIX regular expression.

You can specify the point to stop, as well, by providing a second value as part of a comma-separated string. Make sure there's no space between the start, the comma, and the second value. The second value can be another line number, a regular expression, or a number with a plus (+) or minus (-) before it.

The plus sign shows the start plus the number of lines; the minus sign adjusts the start to show the number of lines before the start. Remember that the plus and minus are zero-indexed. For example, -L 10,+10 shows lines 10 through 19, not lines 10 through 20.

Git can track content that moves around in a file or is copied from one file to another. You can use git blame to show content that has moved around by adding the -M parameter.

You can also track changes copied from another file by using the -C parameter. It checks the changes in the file against other changes in the repository to see whether it was copied from somewhere else.

➤ Display file with entire line-by-line commit information.

```
prompt> git blame some/file
```

➤ Start the output of blame at line 10.

```
prompt> git blame -L 10 some/file
```

➤ Limit the output of blame to lines 10 through 20.

```
prompt> git blame -L 10,20 some/file
... or ...
prompt> git blame -L 10,+11 some/file
... or ...
prompt> git blame -L 20,-11 some/file
```

➤ Show ten lines of output from blame starting at a POSIX regular expression.

```
prompt> git blame -L "/def to_s/",+10 some/file
```

➤ Check the history to see whether the change was moved within the file, and display that information.

```
prompt> git blame -M some/file
```

➤ Check the history to see whether the change was copied from somewhere else or moved around within the file, and display that information.

```
prompt> git blame -C some/file
```

Related Tasks:

• Task 30, *Viewing the Log*, on page 92
• Task 32, *Comparing Differences*, on page 96

Part VII

Fixing Things

As we discussed earlier, Git breaks the process of committing a change and sharing that same change into two separate processes. The benefit of that separation comes into sharp focus when you need to fix something.

Every commit in Git can be changed. You should avoid making changes to commits you've shared to avoid potential conflicts with other developers. Keeping that in mind, you can adjust commits as much as you want.

Covered in this part:

- You need to fix a typo, you forgot to run the unit tests before committing and accidentally broke them, or you found a bug after the commit. You learn how to fix these issues in Task 35, *Fixing Commits*, on page 106.
- You can undo a commit after you've shared your changes by reverting it—applying the reverse of a commit as a new commit. You learn how to do this in Task 36, *Reverting Commits*, on page 108.
- You can reset your current HEAD to any other commit in the repository and start working from there. In practice, it's most useful to undo one or more of the most recent commits. We cover this in Task 37, *Resetting Staged Changes and Commits*, on page 110.
- Sometimes you don't need to fix a commit; you need to remove it entirely. You learn how to do that in Task 38, *Erasing Commits*, on page 112.
- Fixing and removing commits is the easy part. Most issues are bugs in your code. Git provides an excellent tool for isolating the commit (or commits) that introduced a bug. You learn about it in Task 39, *Finding Bugs with bisect*, on page 114.
- Finally, all of this rewriting can cause issues if you're not careful. One of Git's mandates is to *not* lose code, though, so it provides the reflog to help you recover. You learn how to navigate it in Task 40, *Retrieving "Lost" Commits*, on page 116.

<table>
<tr><td>35</td><td>**Fixing Commits**</td></tr>
</table>

35   Fixing Commits

One of the advantages of Git is the ability to "fix" commits. Fixing changes can be as simple as fixing typos that got committed, fixing a bug you didn't catch because you hadn't run your unit tests yet, or doing something as complex as rearranging an entire series of commits so they are ordered more logically.

git commit --amend is the way to fix the most recent commit. It comes in handy for those simple fixes that you catch right away. It is a convenience wrapper around using git reset --soft HEAD^ (see Task 37, *Resetting Staged Changes and Commits*, on page 110) and git commit -c ORIG_HEAD. You can use the -C parameter with --amend when you want to reuse the original commit message.

You can use git rebase -i to replay the history of your repository and stop at certain points. Run the command, provide it with the parent of the commit you want to edit, and then mark that commit as "edit." Git stops at that point and then lets you work on your repository as if it were the previous commit (see Task 28, *Controlling How You Replay Commits*, on page 82).

You can fix typos, remove some buggy code, or do anything else you would normally do with the previous commit. Then, call git rebase --continue so Git can finish rebasing the rest of the history.

It's worth noting again: be careful when rewriting history. Feel free to rewrite to your heart's content until you share your work. After that, only rewrite when you have no other option available.

➤ Amend the previous commit.

Make the changes you want and stage those changes, and then use this:

```
prompt> git commit --amend
... launch editor ...
```

➤ Amend the previous commit, and keep the same log message.

```
prompt> git commit --amend -C HEAD
[master 38ec64e] update the README
 1 files changed, 5 insertions(+), 0 deletions(-)
```

➤ Fix the previous commit by removing it entirely.

```
prompt> git reset --hard HEAD^
HEAD is now at 68f3164 use json if available
```

➤ Use interactive rebase to edit a commit other than the last one.

This command allows you to rewrite history by changing commits. In this example, say you want to edit the third commit before HEAD:

```
prompt> git rebase -i HEAD~3
... launches editor, mark the first commit (the one you want
... to change) as "edit" instead of "pick", then save
... and exit your editor
...
... make the change you want to your commit, then:
prompt> git commit --amend
prompt> git rebase --continue
```

Related Tasks:

<table>
<tr><td>36</td><td>Reverting Commits</td></tr>
</table>

Sometimes we make mistakes. A commit that wasn't supposed to be shared gets pushed to a public repository, a commit has a bug that can't be fixed and needs to be undone, or maybe you just don't need that code any longer. These cases all call for git revert.

The git revert command does just what you might expect. It reverts a single commit by applying a reverse commit to the history.

You can call git revert with just a commit ID. Git launches the editor with the commit message already filled out. It follows this pattern:

```
Revert "some commit message"

This reverts commit <some commit hash>.
```

You can edit this message to be whatever you want. You can use the --no-edit parameter to tell Git to use the default message without passing it through the editor if the default is sufficient.

Sometimes you need to revert several commits to completely undo a change. You can use --no-commit, or you can use -n to tell Git to perform the revert but stop short of committing the change. This lets you combine all the revert commits into one commit, which is useful if you need to revert a feature that spans several commits. Make sure that you revert commits in reverse order—the newest commit first. Otherwise, you might confuse Git by trying to revert code that doesn't exist yet.

You can use git revert to undo commits that you don't want or need any longer, but it does leave a trace. In most cases, you don't want commits "disappearing" from your repository. For those instances where you don't want a record of your commit at all, see Task 38, *Erasing Commits*, on page 112.

➤ Revert a particular commit.

```
prompt> git revert <commit id>
... example ...
prompt> git revert de3245fa
Finished one revert.
... launches editor ...
[master 743d2ef] Revert "simplify this code a bit"
 1 files changed, 1 insertions(+), 1 deletions(-)
```

➤ Revert a particular commit, and use the default message.

```
prompt> git revert --no-edit <commit id>
... example ...
prompt> git revert --no-edit de3245fa
Finished one revert.
[master 3a26b89] Revert "simplify this code a bit"
 1 files changed, 1 insertions(+), 1 deletions(-)
```

➤ Revert a commit, but don't commit the change.

```
prompt> git revert --no-commit <commit id>
Finished one revert.
... or ...
prompt> git revert -n <commit id>
Finished one revert.
```

Related Tasks:

- Task 35, *Fixing Commits*, on page 106
- Task 37, *Resetting Staged Changes and Commits*, on page 110
- Task 38, *Erasing Commits*, on page 112

| 37 | **Resetting Staged Changes and Commits** |

The git reset command lets you change the HEAD—the latest commit your working tree points to—of your repository. It modifies either the staging area or the staging area and working tree.

Git's ability to craft commits exactly like you want means that you sometimes need to undo changes to the changes you staged with git add. You can do that by calling git reset HEAD <file to change>. This is the most common use of the reset and is like Subversion's svn revert command. Remember not to get the two confused. (For more on git revert, see Task 36, *Reverting Commits*, on page 108.)

You have two options to get rid of changes completely. git checkout HEAD <file(s) or path(s)> is a quick way to undo changes to your staging area and working tree. Be careful with this command, however, because it removes all changes to your working tree. Git doesn't know about those changes since they've never been committed. There's no way to get those changes back once you run this command.

Another command at your disposal is git reset --hard. It is equally destructive to your working tree—any uncommitted changes or staged changes are lost after running it. Running git reset --hard HEAD does the same thing as git checkout HEAD . (with an extra period after HEAD); it just doesn't require a file or path to work.

You can use git reset --hard to remove more than staged changes and changes to your working tree. You can give it any commit ID to tell Git to reset your HEAD to that and move the current branch to that location. For example, if you make two commits and then realize neither should be there, a quick git reset --hard HEAD^^ fixes that.

You can use --soft with git reset. It resets the repository to the commit you specify and stages all of those changes. Any changes you have already staged are not affected, nor are the changes in your working tree.

Finally, you can use --mixed to reset the working tree without staging any changes. This also unstages any changes that are staged.

➤ Reset staged changes, but don't erase any changes.

```
prompt> git reset HEAD
Unstaged changes after reset:
M       dolt/__init__.py
... to reset just certain file(s) ...
prompt> git reset HEAD <file1> [<file2> <and so on>]
```

➤ Completely undo the last commit.

Warning: Be careful with this command; it overwrites the changes in any files in your working tree.

```
prompt> git checkout HEAD <file or path to reset>
prompt>
```

➤ Completely remove the last three commits.

Remember, --hard erases any uncommitted changes in your working tree. Git doesn't know about those, so you can't get them back.

```
prompt> git reset --hard HEAD^^^
... or ...
prompt> git reset --hard HEAD~3
HEAD is now at 5eada39 add basic read-only version of api wrapper
```

➤ Reset last commit and stage the changes.

This is useful if the commit has a lot changes, and only a few files and /or paths need to be altered before committing the changes again.

```
prompt> git reset --soft HEAD^
prompt>
```

➤ Undo the last change to HEAD.

```
prompt> git reset ORIG_HEAD
Unstaged changes after reset:
M       dolt/apis/external.py
... if you want to completely remove any changes ...
prompt> git reset --hard ORIG_HEAD
HEAD is now at 99a7a58 fix params_template
```

Related Tasks:

38 Erasing Commits

You can tell Git to erase commits. This is contradictory to most version control systems, but you can treat any commit that you haven't already shared with the rest of the world as something that can be adjusted as necessary.

A word of caution before we get into specifics, though. Don't delete commits that you've shared without a very good reason. Deleting commits causes the history to be rewritten, causing the ripple effect problems like a git rebase. If you've shared commits, your best bet is git revert (see Task 36, *Reverting Commits*, on page 108).

You can use git rebase a couple of different ways to handle deletes. First, you can add the -i parameter to go into an interactive rebase. Once launched, delete the line (or lines) for the commit you don't want to keep, save and exit the editor, and you're off.

Second, you can use --onto to tell Git to rebase onto the commit you want to get rid of. You must specify three parameters: first, you specify the commit you want to start on (the commit before the commit you want to delete); second, you specify the commit before the one you want to start at again; third, you specify the final commit you want available.

Dissecting the command from the opposite page, you're telling Git you want to rebase HEAD (HEAD^ through HEAD, or the last commit) onto c2d2245.

You can also use git reset to remove any number of the latest commits off the end of your repository. You can use --hard to remove the changes from both your index and your working tree, but be careful. This deletes any changes you have in your working tree. git stash (see Task 26, *Temporarily Hiding Changes*, on page 78) is a good idea if you have changes you want to hang on to.

Remember, you can always use git reflog (see Task 40, *Retrieving "Lost" Commits*, on page 116) if one of these commands goes awry. Be mindful of your working tree, though. It warrants repeating: git reset --hard deletes uncommitted changes from your working tree, and those uncommitted changes can't be retrieved.

➤ Erase with an interactive rebase.

prompt> **git rebase -i <commit to erase>^**

For example, to erase commit c2d2245, use this:

prompt> **git rebase -i c2d2245^**
```
... launches editor ...
```

Delete the line that contains the c2d2245 commit, and then save and exit the editor so git rebase can run.

➤ Erase with git rebase --onto.

For example, imagine these commits in your repository:

```
  c2d2245
  /      2245d2c
 /      /
o--o--o--o
     \   \
      \   HEAD
     224cd25
```

Use the following to delete commits 224cd25 and 2245d2c:

prompt> **git rebase --onto c2d2245 HEAD^ HEAD**
```
First, rewinding head to replay your work on top of it...
Applying: add API object for interacting with remote API
```

And after the rebase is successful, the branch looks like this:

```
  c2d2245
  /
o--o
    \
     HEAD
```

➤ Erase the last commit.

prompt> **git reset --hard HEAD^**

Related Tasks:

- Task 16, *Rewriting History by Rebasing,* on page 48
- Task 36, *Reverting Commits,* on page 108
- Task 40, *Retrieving "Lost" Commits,* on page 116

39   Finding Bugs with bisect

Unit tests, code review, pair programming, and any number of practices help limit the number of bugs in your code. We all end up having to track down bugs, though. It's part of software development. git bisect helps you limit the time you spend on this unpleasant task by helping you search through your repository's history for the commit that introduced the bug.

git bisect works by dividing and conquering. You know that a particular commit has a bug in it, or is *bad*. You also know that a particular point in the past didn't have that bug in it, or is *good*.

bisect takes the remaining commits, divides them in half, and sets your working tree to that midway point in the history. You can check your repository for the bug and mark it as either good or bad. Repeat until you narrow the list of possible commits down to the commit that introduced the bug.

You can skip a commit if there's no way to test it. Be careful skipping commits, however. Skipping too many can make it impossible for Git to know which commit caused the bug.

After you've found the commit with the bug and determined how to fix it, you need to move back to the original branch where you started. git bisect reset takes care of that.

You can automate the process of marking a commit as good or bad with a script. It can be any shell script. The script must use its exit status code to mark whether the commit it is testing is good, is bad, or should be skipped. There are three possible exit code status that cause bisect to mark a commit as good, as bad, or as skipped:

- 0 to mark as good
- 1 or greater to mark as bad
- 125 to skip

Git changes your working tree between each test, so make sure that the script you give to git bisect run is independent of the repository history. Create the simplest possible test and put it outside of your working tree, and then use it there so git bisect doesn't accidentally overwrite it.

➤ Use bisect to narrow down the buggy commit.

```
prompt> git bisect start
prompt> git bisect bad
prompt> git bisect good <some commit id>
... mark each commit as good or bad until you
... have narrowed the list of commits down to the
... commit with that introduces the bug
... once you've found the commit and figured out
... how to address it, run the following to return
... back to the branch you started at
prompt> git bisect reset
```

➤ Use a shortcut to start bisect with HEAD being bad.

```
prompt> git bisect start HEAD <some good commit id>
... continue as above
```

➤ Use an automated script to test commits.

```
prompt> git bisect start HEAD <some good commit id>
prompt> git bisect run /path/to/test/script
... once you've figured out the fix
prompt> git bisect reset
```

➤ Find a bug in the history with bisect.

The commit to the right is HEAD, and the commit to the left is known to be good. git bisect cuts the repository in half, and through a process of elimination shows that HEAD^ is the commit that introduced the bug. Now, imagine there were 100 commits separating HEAD and the last known good commit!

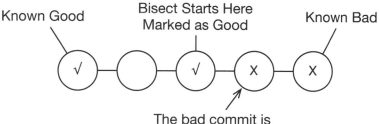

Related Tasks:

40   Retrieving "Lost" Commits

Rebasing commits causes the history of your repository to change. Ever wonder what happens if you accidentally delete the wrong commit in an interactive rebase? The commit—the point in the repository that recorded the change—is still stored in your repository, but it's orphaned. You can use the reflog to find that commit, even though the normal Git log doesn't show it.

The Git reflog tracks every time the tip of a branch changes. The tip is the commit that a particular branch points to. Back in Part III, *Organizing Your Repository with Branches and Tags*, we talked more about branches and how they are pointers to commits. Each time you commit a change to a branch, the branch is updated to point to that new commit, and the change is logged in the reflog.

During normal Git usage, you don't need to concern yourself with the reflog. It's handy for fixing mistakes, however.

For example, you run an interactive rebase (discussed in more detail in Task 28, *Controlling How You Replay Commits*, on page 82) and a few days later realize that you accidentally removed the wrong commit during the rebase. Catching it right after the fact means you can use git reset ORIG_HEAD, but since you didn't, your options are limited to one: using the reflog.

Running git reflog, you can find the commit before you ran your rebase and check it out directly. From there, you can determine the commit IDs for the missing commit, switch to your current branch, and cherry-pick the change back into your current branch.

Also available are the subcommands delete and expire, which delete specific reflog entries and expire entries beyond a certain point, respectively. Under most normal circumstances, you don't need to use either.

Rewriting history is a powerful part of the Git toolkit. The reflog helps keep you from hurting yourself too much.

➤ View the reflog.

prompt> **git reflog**

➤ Retrieve a lost commit.

First, let's "lose" a few commits:

```
prompt> mkdir /work/tmp-repo && cd /work/tmp-repo
prompt> git init
Initialized empty Git repository in /work/tmp-repo/.git/
... add files a, b, c, d to the repository so we have some commits ...
prompt> for i in a b c d
  do echo "simple $i" >> $i && git add $i && git commit -m "simple $i"
  done
... output from Git ...
prompt> git rebase -i HEAD~2
... delete the "simple b" commit ...
Successfully rebased and updated refs/heads/master.
prompt> git log --oneline
4325c46 simple c
4b2a2ba simple a
... re-run the for loop above to add a few new commits ...
```

You can see that you've deleted the =simple b commit. Now you can save it with git reflog:

```
prompt> git reflog
7ab141b HEAD@{0}: commit: simple e
... and so on, and so on ...
4b2a2ba HEAD@{3}: checkout: moving from master to 4b2a2ba
e563dcc HEAD@{4}: commit: simple c
2b469ed HEAD@{5}: commit: simple b
prompt> git cherry-pick 2b469ed
Finished one cherry-pick.
[master fcc3a79] simple b
 1 files changed, 1 insertions(+), 0 deletions(-)
 create mode 100644 b
```

Related Tasks:

Part VIII

Moving Beyond the Basics

At this point you have learned all of the main topics you need to become a proficient Git user. There are a handful of commands that you'll only need to use occasionally.

Covered in this part:

- You may need to export the current state of your repository without the entire history. You learn how to do that in Task 41, *Exporting Your Repository*, on page 122.

- Git attempts to remain as fast as possible, sometimes at the cost of storage efficiency. Task 42, *Doing Some Git Housekeeping*, on page 124 shows you the commands to run to recalculate your repository's internal structure and save some disk space.

- Many developers are still working in an environment where Subversion is their company's version control system of choice. Git provides bidirectional support for SVN—it can both read from and write to an SVN server. You learn about that in Task 43, *Syncing with Subversion*, on page 126.

- Finally, we've talked about repositories exclusively in the context of repositories with a working tree, but there is another type of repository: a bare repo. These are used for sharing changes via pushing and pulling to and from. They're covered in Task 44, *Initializing Bare Repositories*, on page 128.

Now, let's start off with exporting your repository.

41   Exporting Your Repository

Sharing your repository with other developers is a matter of giving them access to read your public repository, but sometimes you need to give access to content you're tracking to people who don't use Git: clients, customers, or business partners of a less tech-savvy variety. You can export the contents of your repository at a particular point to share with these people using the git archive command.

It's important to remember you are exporting only one point in the history of your repository, not the entire history. Some people look at an export as a backup of their repository. This is not the correct way to do a backup in Git. Each clone of your repository has the entire history, so push your repository to a remote repository on some other computer. Backup finished.

You can specify the point you want to export as either a commit ID, HEAD or some other special commit name, a branch, or a tag. You can also specify a relative revision if you want to export the parent of a certain commit.

Provide a --prefix parameter with a trailing slash when using git archive. That tells Git to put the contents of the archive in its own directory within the archive so it's expanded into its own directory when you uncompress it.

git archive exports in either a .tar format or a .zip format. You can specify which you prefer with --format. You can skip the --format parameter if you provide either --output or -o; Git uses the file extension from the file provided to it to determine which type it should export.

You can also pipe the output through other commands to modify the output if you don't use the --output parameter. The most common use is piping the output through gzip or bzip2 with | gzip > some-file.tar.gz. That turns the tar file into a gzipped tar file. You can also pipe a zip file to gzip, but that would be redundant and repetitive.[18]

You can also export individual directories of your repository in addition to exporting the entire repository. You do this by specifying the revision you want to export and adding a colon and the name of the directory you want to export.

---

18.   I really don't recommend doing that, just in case the geek humor didn't make it through in print.

➤ Create a tar.gz file of the latest changes in master.

```
prompt> git archive --format=tar \
        --prefix=my-project-latest/ \
        HEAD | gzip > my-project-latest.tar.gz
prompt>
... or ...
prompt> git archive --prefix=my-project-latest \
        --output my-project-latest.tar && \
        gzip my-project-latest.tar
prompt>
```

➤ Create a zip of the repository at tag v1.0.2.

```
prompt> git archive --format=zip \
        --prefix=my-project-1.0.2/ \
        v1.0.2 > my-project-1.0.2.zip
prompt>
... or ...
prompt> git archive --prefix=my-project-1.0.2/ \
        v1.0.2 -o my-project-1.0.2.zip
prompt>
```

➤ Export one directory.

```
prompt> git archive --format=zip \
        --prefix=my-project/ \
        HEAD:<some directory> > my-project.zip
prompt>
```

Related Tasks:

• Task 3, *Creating a New Repository*, on page 8

42   Doing Some Git Housekeeping

One of Git's key advantages is its speed. Keeping it fast requires some tuning, however. The git gc command provides the tuning tool.

git gc performs several housecleaning tasks. First, it removes any "loose objects" in the repository over a certain age. All of those commits you remove via git rebase, git reset, and so on, are still tracked by Git; they're just orphaned.

Second, it recalculates the deltas. Deltas are the differences between two pieces of content in the repository. Many times the first pass at creating the delta is not the most efficient. Recalculating the deltas with the help of hindsight allows Git to combine like deltas to reduce the size of the repository and decrease the time Git spends looking for information in the repository.

Periodic running of git gc helps keep the repository in top shape. Providing it with the --aggressive parameter tells Git to focus on making the repository as efficient as possible, instead of trying to run the command as quickly as possible.

Git is configured by default to remove loose objects that are older than the gc.pruneExpire values. The default value is two weeks, but you can change this using git config. You can also change it by providing a value to git gc via the --prune=<some value> parameter. This takes the standard time values.

Many of the commands that cause the repository history to become unruly automatically call git gc for you. The most notable is git svn rebase. Older versions of Git required that you run git gc manually to keep the repository size in check. It's still a good idea to run git gc from time to time, though, to make sure your repository is in top shape.

➤ Run garbage collection.

prompt> **git gc**
Counting objects: 3048, done.
Delta compression using up to 2 threads.
Compressing objects: 100% (2564/2564), done.
Writing objects: 100% (3048/3048), done.
Total 3048 (delta 2041), reused 667 (delta 476)
Removing duplicate objects: 100% (256/256), done.

➤ Run garbage collection in the most size-optimized way.

prompt> **git gc --aggressive**
Counting objects: 3048, done.
Delta compression using up to 2 threads.
Compressing objects: 100% (2564/2564), done.
Writing objects: 100% (3048/3048), done.
Total 3048 (delta 2041), reused 667 (delta 476)
Removing duplicate objects: 100% (256/256), done.

➤ Remove "loose objects" that are older than a week.

prompt> **git gc --prune="1 week"**
Counting objects: 244, done.
Delta compression using up to 2 threads.
Compressing objects: 100% (228/228), done.
Writing objects: 100% (244/244), done.
Total 244 (delta 109), reused 0 (delta 0)

Related Tasks:

- Task 16, *Rewriting History by Rebasing,* on page 48

43   Syncing with Subversion

One of Git's key advantages over other DVCSs early on was its ability to communicate with Subversion through git-svn. Though other DVCSs now have integration with Subversion to varying degrees, Git still leads the pack.

git-svn is installed by default on most systems, but on Ubuntu and other Linux-based systems that break up software into individual packages. you do need to install it separately (see Task 1, *Installing Git*, on page 4).

You can clone a Subversion repository with a standard layout[19] by using git svn clone -s and providing Git with the repository URL. You can use --trunk, --tags, and --branches to provide Git with a custom location for your trunk, tags, and branches.

Creating a clone is all you need to do if you're migrating to Git from Subversion, but Git can continue to talk to Subversion if you're not making the switch.

There is no direct git svn update available on Subversion clones. Instead, you use git svn rebase to update your local branch with the upstream changes in Subversion. This fetches the changes from Subversion and then rebases your local branch against the upstream changes.

Remember, using rebasing commits (whether with git rebase or through git svn rebase) comes at a potential cost. git-svn requires a rebase to keep track of which commits are in Subversion and which are only in Git. Because of this, it's not a good idea to share changes directly via Git clones of Subversion repositories. Use Subversion for sharing changes.

You can push changes back upstream to a Subversion repository with git svn dcommit. You can add the -n parameter if you want to see what commits will be sent upstream without actually sending them.

The output from any of the git svn commands could take up several pages of output, so I haven't included any output here.

---

19.   http://svnbook.red-bean.com/en/1.5/svn.tour.importing.html#svn.tour.importing.layout

➤ Create a Git clone of a standard Subversion repository.

prompt> `git svn clone -s svn://example.com/repo`

➤ Perform the equivalent of an svn update.

prompt> `git svn rebase`

➤ Push changes back to upstream Subversion repository.

prompt> `git svn dcommit`

Or, to see what commits would be sent back upstream, use this:

prompt> `git svn dcommit -n`

Related Tasks:

• Task 16, *Rewriting History by Rebasing,* on page 48

44   Initializing Bare Repositories

Most Git repositories that you work with have both the repository metadata (the files located in the .git/ directory) and a working tree (the files that you interact with). Repositories that are meant to pushed to and pulled from, however, are generally created as bare repositories —repositories that don't have a working tree.

You use a bare repository to push your changes to. You generally need only one, but you can have as many as your situation might require. For example, you might need to create two, each one on different servers, so a different set of people can access it. You need to make sure to remember to push to both repositories, though.

Using these repositories helps you separate the act of committing changes and the act of sharing those changes. You keep your local repository private—no one can read directly to it, and no one can push to it. You use a remote repository as a place to share your changes with everyone else.

A bare repository works just like a normal repository, except it doesn't have a copy of the working tree. All of the files that are present in the .git/ of your normal repository are present in the directory where your bare repository lives.

By convention, bare repositories should end in .git. For example, call your bare repository widget.git if its name is widget.

To share your repository, place it somewhere that other people can access it. This could be a network file system, on a directory with proper read permissions on a remote server, or even on an HTTP server. You can also make it accessible via the git daemon so it is accessible via the git protocol.

Most third-party hosting solutions, such as GitHub[20] or Gitorious,[21] handle the creation of the bare repository for you. You only have to push the changes to the repository they create. Likewise, if you use Gitosis,[22] it handles the creation of a bare repository for you.

You can use the git clone --mirror command if you want to clone an existing repository and populate it with the commits from that remote repository. This is useful for creating local copies of a repository to interact with and possibly share, without exposing your private local repository.

---

20.   http://github.com/
21.   http://gitorious.com/
22.   http://eagain.net/gitweb/?p=gitosis.git

➤ Initialize a bare repository.

```
prompt> git init --bare /path/to/some/repo.git
Initialized empty Git repository in /path/to/some/repo.git
```

➤ Create a bare repository copy of a remote repository.

```
prompt> git clone --mirror <remote repository>
... example ...
prompt> git clone --mirror /work/repo
Cloning into bare repository repo.git...
done.
```

Related Tasks:

- Task 4, *Creating a Local Copy of an Existing Repository*, on page 10
- Task 19, *Adding and Removing Remotes*, on page 60
- Task 21, *Retrieving Remote Changes, Part II*, on page 64
- Task 22, *Sending Changes to Remotes*, on page 66

APPENDIX 1

Glossary

- ^: Adding a caret to any commit name (a commit ID, branch name, or tag) tells Git to use that commit, minus one. You can add multiple carets: HEAD^^ means HEAD minus two, and so on.

- ~#: The tilde followed by a number is used with a commit name (a commit ID, branch name, or tag) to specify the commit located at that point minus the number: HEAD~2 means two commits before HEAD, and so on.

- *amend*: Applies the commit that is being made to the previous commit to *amend* it.

- *bare repository*: A repository without a working tree. Generally used for repositories that are meant to be pushed and pulled to and from.

- *blame*: An annotated view of a file (or portion of a file) that shows what commit a change was made in, when that commit happened, and who made it.

- *branch*: A separate line of history within the repository stored as a pointer to a particular commit.

- *check out* or *checkout*: The act of taking a branch or files from the repository and checking it out into the working tree.

- *cherry-pick*: Taking one commit and applying it to the current branch.

- *commit*: The individual points in time that your repository tracks. Each commit in Git tracks who made it, when it was made, the changes that were made, and what commit (or commits) are its direct parents.

- *commit ID*: The ID for each commit is an SHA-1 hash based on the data that makes up a commit. Any change to the commit causes a different commit ID to be generated. Each commit provides its own integrity check through its ID.

- *commit message*: A plain-text message that is stored with the commit. It is used to convey what the commit did and why. By convention, Git breaks commit messages into two parts. The first line is considered the subject, followed by an empty line, followed by the body of the commit message.

- *conflict*: See *merge conflict*.

- *diff*: Describes the differences between two (or more) versions of a file or files.

- *fast-forward merge*: A merge that moves the pointer of a branch to another point in the future without creating a merge commit.

- *fetch*: Retrieving commits from a remote repository and storing them in the local repository.

- *HEAD*: The latest point in your repository that your working tree currently points to.

- *index*: See *staging area*.

- *interactive rebase*: Same as rebase, except Git pauses before the rebase is started and allows you to modify the commits that are being applied, modify the order in which they are applied, and specify which commits should be stopped at so they can be edited.

- *log*: A reverse chronological output of all the commits that, by default, include the committer, commit date, commit ID, and commit message.

- *master*: Refers to the name of the default branch where the majority of development happens in Git.

- *merge*: Bringing the contents of two separate branches into sync by merging them together. This can happen by any number of merge strategies, the most common of which are a fast-forward merge and a recursive merge.

- *merge commit*: A commit with multiple parents used to signify a merging of two or more branches. Merge commits are generally created by recursive merges.

- *merge conflict*: A conflict that happens when two commits attempt make changes that cannot be reconciled by automated means. This generally happens during a merge or while replaying commits during a rebase.

- *non-fast-forward merge*: See *recursive merge*.

- *ORIG_HEAD*: Refers to the location of HEAD before making any changes bigger than a simple commit, such as running git rebase, git reset, or git merge.

- *origin*: The default name for your main remote repository.

- *patch*: The differences between two states of a file along with metadata explaining which file or files were modified.

- *patch mode*: An interactive mode of staging files via git add or git stash that allows you to stage portions of the change rather than the entire file.

- *pull*: The act of fetching changes from a remote repository and merging them into your local branch via git pull. This can be done with a standard merge or via a rebase.

- *push*: The act of sending commits to a remote repository. Generally used when sending your changes to a repository that others can access.

- *rebase*: Replaying one or more commits on top of another point in the history of the repository. Generally used between branches, often where the point you are rebasing against is a remote branch.

- *recursive merge*: A merge where a merge commit is created.

- *reflog*: A log of all changes to the point of a branch (for example, new commits, checkouts, rebases, and so on). Useful for fixing bad rebases.

- *refspec*: References to a particular point inside the repository. Used to refer to branches, it follows the <source>:<destination> schema. Normally used with git pull and git push. When pulling, the source is the remote branch, and the destination is the local branch; when pushing, the source is the local branch, and the destination is the remote branch.

- *remote*: Shorthand for *remote repository*, which refers to repositories other than your own local one.

- *repository*: The place where all your codes and the changes to it—commits—live.

- *revert*: A reverse commit, used to track when a commit was undone.

- *revision*: A particular commit, identified by a commit ID. See *commit* and *commit ID*.

- *stage*: To add a one or more changes to the staging area to be committed.

- *staging area*: The place that sits between the repository and your working tree. You must stage your changes here before they are committed to the repository.

- *stash*: To put all changes in the working tree into a temporary holding area to be reapplied or discarded later. Useful when running rebase, which requires a clean working tree.

- *tag*: A mark of significance within the repository when used as a noun. The act of creating a tag when used as a verb.

- *working tree*: Your copy of a particular point in the repository's history—normally the very last commit, or HEAD—that exists on the file system. This is where you edit the files in your project.

Feel the Power

The command line remains the ultimate power tool for developers, and now your Ruby apps can take full advantage of this environment. And while we're tweaking environments, how about starting with your Mac?

Speak directly to your system. With its simple commands, flags, and parameters, a well-formed command-line application is the quickest way to automate a backup, a build, or a deployment and simplify your life.

David Bryant Copeland
(200 pages) ISBN: 9781934356913. $33
http://pragprog.com/titles/dccar

Exploit secret settings and hidden apps, push built-in tools to the limit, radically personalize your Mac experience and tweak your system so it's just right for you. Every one of these 300 quick and easy tips, tricks, hints and hacks in *Mac Kung Fu* makes "it just works" even better. Become the ultimate Mac user, working faster, smarter, and simply have lots more fun with your Apple computer.

Keir Thomas
(300 pages) ISBN: 9781934356821. $35
http://pragprog.com/titles/ktmack

Welcome to the New Web

You need a better JavaScript and better recipes that professional web developers use every day. Start here.

CoffeeScript is JavaScript done right. It provides all of JavaScript's functionality wrapped in a cleaner, more succinct syntax. In the first book on this exciting new language, CoffeeScript guru Trevor Burnham shows you how to hold onto all the power and flexibility of JavaScript while writing clearer, cleaner, and safer code.

Trevor Burnham
(136 pages) ISBN: 9781934356784. $29
http://pragprog.com/titles/tbcoffee

Modern web development takes more than just HTML and CSS with a little JavaScript mixed in. Clients want more responsive sites with faster interfaces that work on multiple devices, and you need the latest tools and techniques to make that happen. This book gives you more than 40 concise, tried-and-true solutions to today's web development problems, and introduces new workflows that will expand your skillset.

Brian P. Hogan, Chris Warren, Mike Weber, Chris Johnson, Aaron Godin
(325 pages) ISBN: 9781934356838. $35
http://pragprog.com/titles/wbdev

Go Beyond with Rails and NoSQL

There's so much new to learn with Rails 3 and the latest crop of NoSQL databases. These titles will get you up to speed on the latest.

Thousands of developers have used the first edition of *Rails Recipes* to solve the hard problems. Now, five years later, it's time for the Rails 3.1 edition of this trusted collection of solutions, completely revised by Rails master Chad Fowler.

Chad Fowler
(350 pages) ISBN: 9781934356777. $35
http://pragprog.com/titles/rr2

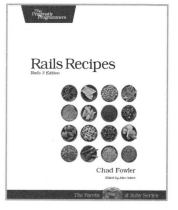

Data is getting bigger and more complex by the day, and so are your choices in handling it. From traditional RDBMS to newer NoSQL approaches, *Seven Databases in Seven Weeks* takes you on a tour of some of the hottest open source databases today. In the tradition of Bruce A. Tate's *Seven Languages in Seven Weeks*, this book goes beyond a basic tutorial to explore the essential concepts at the core of each technology.

Eric Redmond and Jim Wilson
(330 pages) ISBN: 9781934356920. $35
http://pragprog.com/titles/rwdata

Career++

Ready to kick your career up to the next level? Start by growing a significant online presence, and then reinvigorate your job itself.

Technical Blogging is the first book to specifically teach programmers, technical people, and technically-oriented entrepreneurs how to become successful bloggers. There is no magic to successful blogging; with this book you'll learn the techniques to attract and keep a large audience of loyal, regular readers and leverage this popularity to achieve your goals.

Antonio Cangiano
(250 pages) ISBN: 9781934356883. $33
http://pragprog.com/titles/actb

You're already a great coder, but awesome coding chops aren't always enough to get you through your toughest projects. You need these 50+ nuggets of wisdom. Veteran programmers: reinvigorate your passion for developing web applications. New programmers: here's the guidance you need to get started. With this book, you'll think about your job in new and enlightened ways.

Ka Wai Cheung
(250 pages) ISBN: 9781934356791. $29
http://pragprog.com/titles/kcdc

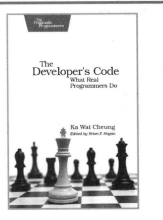